EXCLUSION AND THE CHINESE AMERICAN STORY

EXCLUSION AND THE CHINESE AMERICAN STORY

RACE TO THE TRUTH

Sarah-SoonLing Blackburn

CROWN BOOKS FOR YOUNG READERS
NEW YORK

All rights reserved. Published in the United States by Crown Books for
Young Readers, an imprint of Random House Children's Books, a division of
Penguin Random House LLC, New York.

Crown and the colophon are registered trademarks of
Penguin Random House LLC.

Visit us on the Web! rhcbooks.com

Educators and librarians, for a variety of teaching tools, visit us at
RHTeachersLibrarians.com

Library of Congress Cataloging-in-Publication Data
Names: Blackburn, Sarah-SoonLing, author.
Title: Exclusion and the Chinese American story / Sarah-SoonLing Blackburn.
Description: First edition. | New York: Crown Books for Young Readers,
[2024] | Series: Race to the truth; 3 | Includes bibliographical references. |
Audience: Ages 10 up | Audience: Grades 7–9 | Summary: "The story of
America from the Chinese American perspective"—Provided by publisher.
Identifiers: LCCN 2022060098 (print) | LCCN 2022060099 (ebook) |
ISBN 978-0-593-56763-0 (trade paperback) |
ISBN 978-0-593-56764-7 (library binding) |
ISBN 978-0-593-56774-6 (ebook)
Subjects: LCSH: Chinese Americans—History—Juvenile literature. | Chinese
Americans—Social conditions—Juvenile literature. | United States—Race
relations—History—Juvenile literature.
Classification: LCC E184.C5 B58 2024 (print) | LCC E184.C5 (ebook) |
DDC 973/.04951073—dc23/eng/20221220

The text of this book is set in 12.5-point Adobe Garamond Pro.
Interior design by Michelle Crowe

Printed in the United States of America
10 9 8 7 6 5 4 3 2 1
First Edition

This book is dedicated to those who have crossed oceans and found home.

CONTENTS

A NOTE TO READERS

Dear Reader,

What you have in your hands is a book I wish I'd had when I was growing up. I didn't learn much about Chinese Americans when I was in school. I wasn't taught most of the stories that you are about to encounter in these pages. When I think back on how this made me feel, the word that keeps coming to mind is "invisible." Feeling invisible can make you feel like you don't belong, which isn't a very good feeling. I wrote this book so that maybe someone else can feel a little less invisible.

This book was sometimes difficult to write. I am Chinese American, but it's taken me some time to comfortably claim that identity as my own. When I first started writing, I often wondered whether I was "Chinese American enough." My personal story is different from many of the stories you're about to read. I'm biracial; my dad's family is white, and my mom's family is Chinese. Specifically, my family is Teochew, and they have been in Malaysia for a few generations. I grew up moving between the United States and various parts of Southeast and East Asia, including China, where I attended middle school. Working on this book taught me many important things about myself, and I want to share two of them here. First, my family's story of leaving southern China for Malaysia closely mirrors the stories of families who left southern China for the United States in the late 1800s and early 1900s. I learned that there are many similarities across the diaspora of *overseas Chinese,* a term you will learn in this book, and that there is great power in finding the similarities that lie within experiences that might seem quite different on the surface. Second, I realized that there is no "correct" way to be Chinese American. If you identify as Chinese and you identify as American, then you can identify as Chinese American. It doesn't matter whether your family came to the United States in the 1800s,

1900s, or 2000s. It doesn't matter whether you have two Chinese parents, or you were adopted, or your family composition is something else entirely. I hope that this book shows some of the diversity of what it can mean to be "Chinese American," and I hope that more people feel comfortable claiming that identity with pride, if it makes sense for them.

Another challenge I had while writing this book was trying to honor the histories and experiences of Chinese Americans alongside the histories and experiences of other communities that are often marginalized, particularly Black and Indigenous Americans. I'll be real—people from historically marginalized groups have not always gotten along. There is often anti-Black and anti-Indigenous racism tied up in the history of Chinese Americans, and vice versa. People who look like me have both been harmed by racism and have perpetuated racism. Many of the stories within this book show how both of these things can be true at the same time. Another complication is that, of course, the individual people who make up these various groups are not all the same. As you might have heard, these groups are not monoliths. The people within these groups hold many different opinions, experiences, and feelings about themselves, about each other, and about what it means to be an American. So, I don't think it's very helpful to focus on individual acts of prejudice; instead, as much as possible, I have tried to illustrate the broader structures that have often kept these groups in opposition to one another. The story of Chinese Americans cannot be told without explorations of big, complicated concepts like racial hierarchies, white supremacy, imperialism, and colonialism. I have tried my best to describe these concepts in straightforward terms, and to weave these concepts through the book so that you can recognize how they have existed throughout history and continue to exist today.

One of the concepts I have tried to spotlight is solidarity. Once you realize that there are broader systems that keep many people working against their own and each other's best interests, you start to see these systems everywhere. You also start to see that these systems keep power in the hands of a small group of people, at the expense of poor people, people of color, and historically marginalized people of all kinds. If you're anything like me, you can find these realizations exhausting and depressing. But it doesn't help anything to shrug and give up and say, "Oh well, this is just how it is." The only solution to systems that divide people who are different from one another is to unify with people who are different from ourselves, in spite of those systems. The only solution for the system known as *divide and conquer* is *solidarity*. I hope that this book gives you many examples of what it means to work across differences to advance our collective rights and well-being.

This book does not cover every piece of Chinese American history. There is simply no way to tell the complete history of such a richly diverse group of people in just a small volume. The full history could fill entire libraries. But I've done my best to tell some of the important stories, the lesser-known stories, and the stories that will inspire you to want to learn more. Take this book as a starting point, and then continue to learn. Seek out more books, and seek out other sources, like documentaries, podcasts, and articles. Seek out the stories of elders. May your curiosity be sparked, and may your learning never cease. And may you, too, find ways to uplift the voices and stories of others who have been excluded so that, together, we can create a society in which all of us belong.

In solidarity,
Sarah-SoonLing Blackburn

INTRODUCTION

How much have you learned about Chinese American people or history? If the answer is "very little," you're not alone. Even adults usually answer this question that way, including adults who *are* Chinese American. Chinese American history, and Asian American history in general, is rarely taught in the United States. If you were taught about Chinese American people in school, you probably heard something like "the Chinese came to build the railroads." This is partly true (and you *will* read about railroads in this book!), but it is a vast oversimplification, and it only represents a small fraction of the journeys and reasons that Chinese people have immigrated to and made a home in the United States.

There is so much more to Chinese American history than this single narrative.

When Chinese American stories do show up in textbooks, it's usually just for a paragraph or two. But there are more than five million Chinese American people in the United States today, and this group continues to grow. Chinese Americans have played a part in much more than just a few paragraphs of the broader history and story of the United States, and yet most Americans don't know much or anything at all about Chinese Americans. So whether we identify as Chinese American ourselves or not, we all can benefit from understanding more about Chinese American stories, histories, and experiences.

UNTIL RECENTLY, many United States history books didn't start with Indigenous Americans but with the Italian explorer Christopher Columbus. *Indigenous* means the first people who lived in a region, as opposed to later immigrants. Another common term for Indigenous people is Native people. Today, some scholars believe that around 499 CE a Chinese monk named Hui Shen (sometimes spelled Hoei-Shin) came to the western coast of North America and lived among Indigenous Americans. That is almost *one thousand years* before Christopher Columbus landed in what is now called the Bahamas. These scholars say that Hui Shen wrote about his experiences, sharing descriptions of people and plants that are similar to what would have been found in North America at the time. A few modern anthropologists, or people who study humans and their cultures, even believe that some Indigenous communities of the Americas continue to show evidence of a long-ago interaction with a Chinese person.

Now, most scholars say that this probably never happened. There's more evidence that Hui Shen never came to North America than there is evidence that he did. The reason that this book opens with his story is not to tell you that the story is true, but to tell you something about the ways people like to tell historical stories. You see, every culture has origin stories. Indigenous Americans have origin stories about how their people first came to be on the land that is now the United States. White Americans have origin stories, like Christopher Columbus and the *Mayflower*, establishing centuries of their presence in the Americas. Black Americans, Latine Americans, and every other group of Americans likewise have origin stories. You can read many of these stories in the Race to the Truth series. Whenever you encounter an origin story, take some time to ask yourself a few questions: Where did the story first come from? Who tells the story the most often, and who doesn't tell the story? Does the story affirm a group's right to belong? How is this story used to confirm, deny, or erase other origin stories?

EVEN THOUGH Hui Shen probably didn't travel to North America, his story is a helpful reminder that people have been traveling across the globe and meeting different cultures for centuries. The telling and retelling of Hui Shen's journey as an origin story for Chinese Americans is connected to the very human need to belong. And this story reminds us that Chinese people have probably had contact with the Americas for a lot longer than most of us realize.

AFONG MOY, THE CHINESE LADY

During the earliest years of the United States, most Americans were not allowed to set foot in China. The Chinese emperor Qianlong, who ruled from 1735 to 1796, was concerned that European nations were getting too powerful and having too much influence over China. The United States was a new nation, controlled by white people of European descent. Emperor Qianlong worried that these white Americans would try to take land and power in China just like they had been taking land and power from Indigenous people in North America. Qianlong wanted to limit the movement of Americans and Europeans in China. He created rules keeping white merchants in specific trading areas, like ports.

During these early years of the United States, there were also very few Chinese people who arrived in America. A small number of Chinese men traveled on American merchants' ships to try to find work as laborers in the United States. Most of the early back-and-forth between the two countries was by men who would make the long sea voyage to seek their fortune in the other land. Most of these men had no intention of remaining in the other country permanently, planning instead to return home once they had found the wealth and stability they had been looking for.

THE FIRST STORY we know for sure of a Chinese woman coming to the United States is a tragic one. On October 17, 1834, a ship called *Washington* arrived at New York Harbor. On board the ship was a young woman who would come to be known as Afong Moy. Afong Moy was not the young woman's birth name, but her real name has been lost to history. We also don't know exactly where or when the young woman was born, but scholars have been able to piece together a general idea of the world she probably came from. Afong Moy was about nineteen years old when she arrived in the United States. She probably came from Guangdong Province, a region on the coast of southern China. Almost all trade between the United States and China happened out of the port in the city of Guangzhou, a city that most English-speaking people at the time called Canton. Afong's family probably lived somewhere nearby.

Guangdong Province, with the names used by cities in the region today.

Afong's family was probably middle class. We know this because she had a characteristic that would one day make her famous. Afong Moy had bound feet. The practice of foot-binding had been common in China for hundreds of years, particularly among upper- and middle-class women. Foot-binding was painful. It involved breaking the bones in a girl's foot, then binding the foot tightly in cloth bandages to change its shape. This process would be regularly repeated as the girl grew, so that her feet would remain small and delicate throughout her life. Smaller feet were seen as more beautiful, and bound feet were also a sign of higher status. Women with bound feet had a difficult time standing or walking all day, so it was rarely practiced among farmers or others who had to do hard physical labor in order to survive. Foot-binding was more common in northern China, where most people were of Han ethnicity, than in southern or western China. In Guangdong Province, where Afong's family lived, working-class and poor women and girls rarely had bound feet. Foot-binding was also an expensive process, requiring special herbs, regular unbinding and rebinding, and treatment for the infections that so often ensued.

Because of all the things we know about foot-binding, we can infer that Afong Moy's family probably worked as merchants, but it seems they eventually fell on hard times or weren't very successful at what they did. When Afong was a teenager, her family either sent her or allowed her to leave China to go to the United States. Times were tough for many people in Guangzhou, and some American newspapers claimed that Afong's family had been paid to allow their daughter to leave. Other newspapers thought that Afong Moy was kidnapped and forced to leave her country by American merchants who were trying to get rich. Whatever the case, Afong almost certainly never saw her family again.

Two American merchants, brothers named Francis and Nathaniel Carnes, had a business buying items from China like furniture, art, textiles, and household goods and selling them in the United States. They were in business with a ship captain named Benjamin Obear, who worked with the brothers to come up with a strategy to make their business more successful. Most Americans knew almost nothing about China and might not have been too interested at first in buying Chinese goods, but they were curious about the country. Captain Benjamin Obear and the Carnes brothers thought that a real Chinese woman might help them raise interest in what they were trying to sell. In 1834, the ship

Washington traveled from Guangzhou to New York City carrying Benjamin Obear and his wife, the brothers Francis and Nathaniel, the teenage Afong Moy, and many beautiful Chinese items to be sold to the wealthy people of America's East Coast. Also on the ship was a teenage Chinese boy who could speak both English and Chinese and who would serve as Moy's interpreter. This other teenager's name is also lost to history. The records we have today refer to him only as "Acong."

When Afong Moy first arrived in New York City, the plan was that she would help to sell the Carnes brothers' goods. They would hold exhibitions where Afong would appear in her Chinese clothing and explain the different items to the people who came to see, with the help of Acong the interpreter. The first exhibition, in November 1834, was held at Captain Benjamin Obear's house. The exhibition was a hit, mostly because very few people in New York had ever met someone from China before. They were curious about Afong and the place she'd come from. More exhibitions were quickly scheduled. For the next few years, Afong Moy appeared at museums and exhibit halls up and down the East Coast. In each exhibition, Afong would sit for hours at a time among an artful display of Chinese furniture and other items for sale, which she would describe to the audience through Acong's interpretation. She would be dressed in traditional Chinese clothing and makeup, and she eventually learned a few words of English to use with her audience. Wherever she went, the attendees seemed more interested in the teenage girl from China than they did in what Francis and Nathaniel Carnes had to sell.

Posters advertising these exhibits referred to Afong as "The Chinese Lady" and described her as a "novelty" or a "curiosity." Afong Moy herself had become the highlight of the show, and Benjamin Obear and the Carnes brothers realized that they could make money simply from bringing her on tour. People would come even if the exhibits didn't have Chinese furniture and other goods for sale. Like an animal in a circus, Afong had become an object for Americans to look at. The more exotic and different the men in charge of the exhibitions could make Afong

An advertisement for Afong Moy's exhibition in the Philadelphia newspaper the American Sentinel, *February 17, 1835.*

Moy seem, the more Americans would pay money to come and stare at her, and the greater wealth and influence these men would gain. Thousands of people eventually came to see Afong Moy in the exhibitions. In Washington, D.C., she was even brought to the White House so that President Andrew Jackson could meet the famous "Chinese Lady."

In particular, white American audiences were amazed and fascinated by Afong Moy's bound feet. Seeing an opportunity to bring even larger crowds, Benjamin Obear would place a footstool in front of Afong so that her feet in their tiny shoes could be propped up and on display for the audience. In January 1835, eight physicians in Philadelphia carefully inspected Afong's feet so that they could write about them in newspapers and medical journals. They unwrapped her feet, took measurements, drew sketches, wrote detailed notes, and talked with each other about how strange and fascinating they were. The physicians brought some of their friends to watch the whole thing, and the owners of Afong's exhibition were there watching, too. This must have been a humiliating experience for Afong Moy. A Chinese woman's bound feet were considered private, and to have strangers—especially male strangers—touch, examine, measure, and talk about her feet would have been a big invasion of her privacy. This humiliating experience, including detailed information about Afong's feet, was widely covered in newspapers and magazines across the country. It was even written about in a magazine for American children.

Can you imagine being brought to a completely new land, being the only person of your ethnicity and gender in the whole country, being sent on tour because your existence is seen as strange and exotic to the people of that country, and having intimate details about your body written about and shared all over? Would you feel uncomfortable? Homesick? Angry? Afong Moy must have felt so many different emotions about her experiences in the United States, but she didn't have the platform to share what she thought or felt about it. Today, we don't have any records about what Afong was feeling in her own words, but we can imagine putting ourselves in her place and realize just how alone she must have felt.

In 1836, the posters advertising the Afong Moy exhibition started saying that she was about to leave to return to China. This turned out not to be true. Whether her plans to leave didn't work out or whether the posters' claims were simply lies to draw bigger audiences, Afong would remain in the United States until at least 1850. It's unclear why she stopped working with Benjamin Obear and the Carnes brothers, and she disappears from the historical record for a while. It seems that Afong Moy was eventually abandoned in New Jersey, and when she turned up again in records she was living with a poor widow and her family. It seems that in the missing years, she had experienced significant mistreatment.

We know that by 1847 Afong Moy had started working for P. T. Barnum, the famous American showman and cofounder of the legendary Barnum and Bailey Circus. She was once again on tour as a novelty, appearing alongside a little person who went by the stage name "General Tom Thumb." Onstage, she would sing Chinese songs, demonstrate her use of chopsticks, and, of course, have her bound feet on display in their small shoes. While this was probably better than Afong's years in poverty, P. T. Barnum was not known for his kindness or generosity toward the people he put on display. He selected people he thought others would find strange, and he tried to play up that strangeness to attract more paying customers. It is unlikely that P. T. Barnum helped Afong beyond what he needed to do to keep her profitable. We don't know what happened to Afong Moy after 1850. Some people speculate that she married a Chinese American man, others that she eventually went to Europe to continue appearing in exhibitions. She was never welcomed in the United States but was always treated as a strange novelty. It's unlikely that she ever returned to China.

CHAPTER I

BECOMING CHINESE AMERICAN

What would make you leave your home and undertake a long, uncomfortable, and often dangerous journey across the ocean to an unfamiliar land? In the middle of the 1800s, the first major waves of Chinese people started arriving in a place called California. China and California were not only separated by thousands of miles of ocean, they were separated by differences in language, religion, and history. China was an ancient civilization, while the United States was a very young nation. In fact, California only became a state in 1850. Before the 1850s, the few Chinese people in America, like Afong Moy, were often making the much longer journey to the big cities of America's East Coast. With

Californian statehood, however, the United States seemed just a little bit easier to reach than it had before, even though it was still terribly far away. The Chinese people who immigrated to this new country were leaving behind their homes, their families, and everything else that had been familiar to them before. Most left home with the hope that they would one day return, but there was no guarantee that they ever would. Making the decision to leave must have been an emotionally difficult one.

The journey from China to the United States was also physically difficult. It required spending a month or more on a ship crossing the vast Pacific Ocean, and the voyage was uncomfortable. Most Chinese people who set off for America were not wealthy, and they had to borrow money from friends, family, or money lenders to help pay for their passage. Even with borrowed money, these passengers could only afford to travel in steerage, or the lowest class of travel. Traveling in steerage meant sharing sleeping quarters with the other steerage passengers, often including sharing bunk beds covered with thin straw mattresses. The food on the journey was basic and unappetizing, and the sanitation was awful. Imagine the smells of all the people crammed in together for such a long time with no showers, no modern toilets, and no proper health

Chinese steerage passengers on board the SS China *en route to Hawai'i in 1901.*

care. Many people died on the journey. On one ship that made the journey from Hong Kong to San Francisco during that time period, one out of every five people aboard did not survive the voyage.

Now that you can imagine just how difficult the journey to the United States was for early Chinese Americans, ask yourself this question again: What would make you leave your home and undertake a long, uncomfortable, and often dangerous journey across the ocean to an unfamiliar land? The lure of what might await on the other end would have to seem worth the pain of leaving family, the discomfort of the voyage, and the risk of losing your life.

The lure that finally pushed more Chinese people to take those risks was one that has lured people across human history—the lure of gold, and the better life that might come with it.

GOLD

It was 1848 in what was soon to become the American state of California when a white sawmill worker named James W. Marshall reported finding gold in the foothills of the Sierra Nevada Mountains. The news that a fortune might be hiding in the great mountain range's soil and streams quickly spread around the world. Thousands of people from across North America and the globe made their way to California, arriving from Europe, Latin America, Asia, and even as far away as Australia.

In the early years of the excitement, Native and Indigenous people from the region participated in the search for gold. Soon, however, many of the new settlers wanted the land for themselves. These settlers, sometimes turning to violence and even murder, forced many Native people to leave their lands. They did not want to share the wealth that might still be discovered, and to some of these settlers a Native person's life was not as important as the possibility of digging up a fortune. And yet, the competition for gold grew. More and more people from more parts of the world continued to arrive to try their luck. The California Gold Rush had begun.

IN CHINA, the craze for gold started like this: Merchants had long traveled between the Americas and China to buy and sell goods, but now these merchants also spread tales of a place where gold could be picked up from the land and where poor people were becoming rich overnight. For people living in Guangdong Province on the coast of southern China, the news of gold was especially alluring. China is a large country, and different regions of China have different histories, languages, and ethnic groups. At the time, Guangdong Province was largely made up of people who spoke Chinese dialects—forms of language that are spoken in a certain region or by a certain group— like Taishanese, Cantonese, Teochew, and Hakka.

In the mid-1800s, Guangdong Province and other nearby areas had gone through years of extreme hardship. Flooding and droughts led to crop failures that led to famine. A war between the British and Chinese known as the Opium War had forced many farmers off their land. The Chinese wanted to end the trade in an addictive drug called opium because it was causing harm to too many people, but the British wanted to continue making money through opium. They wanted to keep the large port cities of the region, like Guangzhou, the capital of Guangdong, open to foreign trade. The British ultimately won the Opium War, continuing the traffic of opium through the province and taking the port city of Hong Kong as their own. The challenges of the war had led to high taxes and limited options for the future. All but the richest people were suffering.

When people in Guangdong Province started hearing stories of *Gam Saan* (or "Gold Mountain"), the hardships they might face trying to get there seemed like nothing in comparison to the hardships they were already facing at home. Then, in 1852, a massive crop failure was the last straw for many people. That year more than twenty thousand Chinese people arrived in San Francisco to seek a better life, about ten times as many as had arrived just the previous year. Almost all of these people were men, setting out to seek their fortune by looking for gold. For the next several years, more and more Chinese people arrived in California to try their luck at finding gold. By 1860, about one quarter of all the gold miners in the region were Chinese.

Like most tales of easy riches, however, the stories about Gold Mountain were much better than the reality. Life for Chinese people in California was not easy. While some lucky miners found a fortune in gold, many more barely scratched out a living. They had borrowed money in China to pay for their voyage to California. On top of what it cost to live, the miners had to earn enough to pay back what they had borrowed, plus interest, a fee for borrowing money that has to be repaid to the lender. Whatever gold was left over did not stay in their pockets either, as many miners felt a responsibility to send as much as possible home to their families in China.

A DAY IN THE LIFE of the typical Gold Rush miner was brutal. They woke up at dawn and spent twelve to sixteen hours a day doing the backbreaking work of digging and washing dirt in the hopes of a glimmer of gold. American and European miners had realized that the numbers of Chinese miners would only continue to grow, and many

An illustration of Chinese gold miners using the panning and cradling method.

started to speak out with hatred. They wanted to limit the chances that one of the large gold discoveries would go to the Chinese. Out in the gold fields, each miner had their own section called a claim. If a Chinese miner got lucky by finding gold and did not carefully guard his claim, it would be stolen by someone else. Sometimes Chinese miners had to work for white miners for only a small cut of any profits they might find. More often, Chinese miners had no choice but to work on claims that had already been searched through and abandoned. That meant that the Chinese miners' chances of finding gold were even lower than everyone else's. Most never found anything of much worth.

At the end of the long day of work, miners returned to their camps. Chinese miners tended to live together for protection and for a feeling of familiarity. They were far away from home, in a land with what seemed like strange food and customs. Most Chinese miners didn't speak English. It isn't hard to imagine how homesick they must have felt. By

Seven miners in Auburn Ravine, California, in 1852; three white miners standing to the left, four Chinese miners standing on the right.

living in camps together, the Chinese miners were able to cook familiar foods, speak their native languages, and swap stories about their families with people who would understand.

The Chinese miners created a community with one another. The miners who were fortunate enough to find gold started new businesses. They had learned through hard personal experiences that the United States was not always a friendly place for Chinese people, and they wanted to make the experience a little bit easier for the newest Chinese arrivals. Others had come from wealthier backgrounds in China, making the voyage across the Pacific not in steerage but in their own cabins. These more successful Chinese people formed mutual-aid groups known as *associations* to support the growing Chinese community. You will hear about the associations many more times throughout this book. People from the associations would meet hopeful new miners right as they got off the boats from China. The associations would help these newcomers find somewhere to stay, get what they needed to work in the mines, or find other jobs. The growing Chinese community started to put down roots in the United States, building temples and schools as well as stores and restaurants. Some of these buildings still exist today.

The Bok Kai Temple in Marysville, California, was built during the Gold Rush. It is still an active temple today!

YEE AH TYE, A POWERFUL MAN

In 1852, a man arrived in San Francisco from Guangdong Province. His name was Yee Ah Tye, and he was about twenty years old. Traditionally, Chinese people list their last name first, so his last name was Yee and his first name was Ah Tye. You will see many other names throughout this book that follow the same pattern. Ah Tye spent his first night on American land shivering in the doorway of a building with some of the other new arrivals. But Yee Ah Tye had some different experiences that set him apart from most of his companions. For one thing, he had lived in Hong

Kong, and because Hong Kong was controlled by the British, Ah Tye could speak English. Ah Tye worked as a translator, and he quickly rose in one of the most powerful associations, the Sze Yup Association. Yee Ah Tye was known for being an outgoing leader who would make deals with the white authorities in California, helping to ease the transition for new Chinese arrivals. But Ah Tye also had a dark side to his reputation. A newspaper called the *San Francisco Herald* ran an article describing how he would brutally punish any Chinese arrivals who did not do what he said. He was also taken to court by a Chinese woman who claimed that he was trying to extort money from her, or forcing her to give him money by using threats or other illegal methods.

Perhaps to escape his conflicts in San Francisco, Yee Ah Tye eventually moved to Sacramento, California. Newspaper reports from his time there show how he became one of the most prosperous Chinese people in the state. In 1861, he hosted a Lunar New Year dinner for other wealthy Chinese people as well as important leaders from the white community, like a judge, a doctor, and a lawyer. There were twenty-six courses served for dinner, including bird's nest soup, two kinds of duck, five brands of champagne, and cigars to finish the meal. This kind of feast was out of reach for most Chinese people at the time, but powerful association leaders often ate well. Archaeologists have looked at the sites where association boardinghouses used to stand, and they have found the remains of expensive Chinese fish, multiple species of birds, and a whole lot of pork. Eating pork symbolizes wealth and prosperity to Chinese people, but it was very expensive in California at the time. By looking at what these associations left behind, archaeologists have been able to prove that powerful association leaders like Yee Ah Tye lived a very good life compared to the other early Chinese Americans.

At the end of his life, Yee Ah Tye continued to go against tradition. He had spent most of his life in California, and he decided that he wanted to be buried in the United States. Most Chinese people came to the U.S. to find their fortune and return home to China, not to settle down permanently in their new country. If a Chinese person died in the U.S., most thought it was important that their remains be sent back to China so that their

Yee Ah Tye's gravesite in Oakland, California.

spirit could be in the land of their ancestors. Ah Tye surprised his family by requesting to be buried in this new country, though he incorporated Chinese traditions into his funeral. Chinese people often give offerings of food at funerals or at the burial sites of relatives. In typical fashion, Yee Ah Tye's spirit was sent off with a feast of meat, cakes, fruits, wine, and more.

YEE AH TYE'S CHOICE to be buried in his new country shows how some Chinese people in America were starting to think of themselves as a new sort of person, a Chinese American person. These early Chinese Americans felt a strong connection to their new home, even though this new home didn't always act like it wanted them. During the Gold Rush, white Americans raised concerns about all the foreigners whom they saw as competition, especially miners from Latin America and China. In response, California created taxes that only foreign miners were required to pay. One of these racist taxes, the Foreign Miners' Tax Act of 1850, required that all miners who were not U.S. citizens pay twenty dollars a month to the state of California. White European miners from countries like France, Germany, and Ireland were not required to pay this tax, even though they were also technically "foreigners." Many Latin American miners, unable or unwilling to pay the tax, returned to their home countries. Many Chinese American miners left the mines as well, but they had traveled over a wide ocean and often could not afford to make the journey back to China. Instead, many Chinese people were pushed into cities like Sacramento and San Francisco, where they created the country's first Chinatowns.

In spite of the hardships, the promise of a fortune in gold remained strong, and throughout the 1850s, more Chinese people continued to make their way to California in hopes of striking it rich. The Foreign Miners' Tax Act of 1850 was overturned after less than a year, and thousands of Chinese people returned to the gold mines. The reprieve didn't last for long. Remember that in 1852, ten times as many Chinese people came to the U.S. as came in 1851. If American miners were upset about competition from Chinese miners before, they were even more upset now. The Foreign Miners' License Act of 1852 was passed, and this time Chinese miners were the clear and only target. This new law required that Chinese miners pay about three dollars per month to the state of California—not as much as the twenty dollars required before, but still a lot of money for people with very little to begin with, whose only hope of making it rich lay in finding a big chunk of gold in the dirt and mud of the mines. It's no wonder that most miners never became rich. As mining became less and less appealing, Gold Mountain was no longer the only destination for immigrants from China. Instead, Chinatowns in cities like Sacramento and San Francisco continued to grow, and these became the true center of life for early Chinese Americans.

CHINATOWN

Imagine that it is the late 1800s. You are on the streets of Chinatown in San Francisco. What do you think you would see, smell, and hear?

Looking around, you might not realize at first glance that you were in California. On both sides of the street, you would see buildings that combine Western and traditional Chinese architecture, but most of the signs would be written in Chinese. You would hear Chinese being spoken in the streets. Most of the early Chinese Americans spoke the dialects of Guangdong Province, like Cantonese and Taishanese. If you closed your eyes on the streets of Chinatown and listened, you might think that you were in Hong Kong or Guangzhou!

You would see Chinese temples built by the associations, whose money and influence continued to hold power in the Chinese American community. One of these temples, the Tin How Temple, is the oldest Taoist temple in the United States and is still in use today. The Tin How Temple honors the Chinese sea goddess Mazu. The goddess Mazu is worshipped by many "overseas Chinese," a term sometimes used to describe Chinese people and their descendants who migrated across oceans. Overseas Chinese people can be found across the world in places as far apart as New Zealand, Jamaica, Malaysia, South Africa, and the United States.

A Taoist temple in San Francisco's Chinatown in 1890.

The Chinese Americans who lived in California in the 1800s were part of the early wave of overseas Chinese people. As hunger and conflict prompted more Chinese people to find new homes across the globe, their understandings of who they were and where they belonged continued to evolve. Some overseas Chinese people thought of themselves as fully

Chinese while living in a new land. These people kept their language, clothing, and traditions, only interacting with other Chinese people even in their new countries. Other overseas Chinese people started to think of themselves as more a part of their new country, and worked to *assimilate,* or fit in, within a new culture. They learned new languages, changed their appearance, and converted to new religions, choosing to leave behind their Chinese identity as much as possible.

And still other people found an identity that was more in the middle. For many Chinese people in California, to be Chinese American was to be both Chinese and American— to retain many of their Chinese traditions while adopting new traditions as Americans. These people realized that belonging was not about changing themselves to be more like white Americans. Instead, belonging was about changing the idea of who gets to be an American to begin with and that being American can mean many different things and look many different ways. The activism and work that the early Chinese Americans did to belong changed not just what it meant to be Chinese and American, it changed what it means to be American, period. Their experiences helped to expand the ideas of who could belong in the United States.

• • •

ONE WAY that Chinese Americans built a bridge between their two homes was through food. Food is an important part of Chinese culture, so many of the buildings in Chinatown were grocery stores and Chinese restaurants. Standing on the street in Chinatown, you would see stands outside grocery stores with stacks of ingredients used in traditional Chinese cooking. You would see delicious dishes through restaurant windows. You would smell foods like roast meat, stir-fried vegetables, and fragrant soups. You might also see and smell chop suey, a dish that isn't actually from China.

Chop suey can help us understand how the new Chinese American culture bridged China and the United States. Most people believe it was invented in Chinatowns in the 1880s. Chop suey is a dish of stir-fried meats and vegetables, and it combines Chinese and Western cooking and ingredients. Because of its diverse origins, this new dish tasted delicious to a diverse group of people, including those who'd never tried

San Francisco's Chinatown in 1945, with a sign for chop suey.

Chinese food before. A chop suey craze quickly spread across the United States. Chop suey brought non-Chinese diners to Chinatowns, and by the 1920s you could find chop suey restaurants all across the country. Today, Chinese food is a familiar staple of American cuisine, and many food scholars have remarked that dishes like chop suey are "as American as apple pie." We can think of chop suey as a metaphor for the belonging that Chinese Americans hoped for. Chinese Americans didn't have to change what they ate in order to fit in to their new country. Instead, they expanded what all Americans considered American food and changed what an American family dinner might look like, regardless of race or ethnicity.

THE PERPETUAL FOREIGNER STEREOTYPE

Not all aspects of Chinese American culture were so widely accepted. In Chinatown in the 1800s, you wouldn't only smell food. You would also smell Chinese-operated laundromats, incense, and the natural smells of miners and other people who did physically demanding labor to survive. While these smells might have made some Chinese Americans feel more at home, not everyone in San Francisco agreed. Even as Chinese Americans were feeling more at home in their new country, many people from other groups did not think that Chinese people should belong at all. They thought that Chinese people were untrustworthy and would always be too different to ever fit in. This belief that Chinese people would never belong is known as the *perpetual foreigner stereotype,* and it has continued to linger in how some Americans view Chinese Americans and Asian American people in general, even today.

By looking at how Chinese Americans were treated in California back in the 1800s, we can see just how hurtful the perpetual foreigner stereotype can be. A false belief formed among non-Chinese residents that Chinese people are naturally stinky, dirty, and full of disease. These stereotypes might sound familiar to you because they have reemerged throughout American history, most recently during the Covid-19 pandemic. When diseases like smallpox, cholera, and tuberculosis broke out in San Francisco in the late 1800s, many people were quick to blame the Chinese population, even though these diseases were more likely caused by overcrowding, bad sanitation, and contaminated water. Instead of constructing more housing and building sanitation systems, the city of San Francisco passed something called the Cubic Air Ordinance of 1870. This law claimed to help the population stay healthy by restricting the number of people who could live in the same space, but it was only enforced against the Chinese population. Ironically, so many Chinese people were put in jail for violating the Cubic Air Ordinance that the jails became *more* crowded than the crowded homes that had gotten them in trouble in the first place!

You would see lots of people out on the street in Chinatown. Many of the people wore traditional Chinese clothing, and others wore Western apparel. Most of the Chinese people in the United States at the time were men, and many of them wore their hair in a long braid known as a *queue*. The Manchu people who ruled China during the Qing Dynasty (1644–1912) required other ethnic groups to wear their hair in this way as a symbol of loyalty. Many white Americans were suspicious of people who wore the queue, questioning whether Chinese Americans were more loyal to their old country than their new one, and stereotyping the long hairstyle as less masculine.

A photo of a Chinese American man with a queue, around 1900.

Because of these suspicions, San Francisco lawmakers tried to pass a law in 1873 that would force people in jail to cut their hair to just one inch long. This law was specifically targeted at Chinese people, as opposed to all people who were imprisoned. And remember, an unequal proportion of Chinese people were being imprisoned because of the Cubic Air Ordinance. The new law about hairstyles was called the "Pigtail Ordinance," but the mayor of San Francisco quickly vetoed, or overruled, it. He said, "This order, though general in its terms, in substance and effect, is a special and degrading punishment inflicted upon the Chinese residents for slight offenses and solely by reason of their alienage and race." In other words, he said that the law unfairly targeted Chinese people for no good reason. Unfortunately, his words did not end the widespread prejudice against Chinese men and their hairstyles, and in 1876, the San Francisco Board of Supervisors successfully passed a Pigtail Ordinance.

In spite of these laws, Chinese Americans resisted the racism and discrimination they faced. In 1873, a group of Chinese people in San Francisco made a plea to their city's council, arguing that they deserved to be treated fairly and like they belonged. This plea was eventually published as a document called *The Chinese Question from a Chinese Standpoint,* which read, in part:

Will you listen to a calm, respectful statement of the Chinese question from a Chinese standpoint? Public sentiment is strongly against us . . . All the evils and miseries of our people are constantly pictured in an exaggerated form to the public, and our presence in this country is held up as an evil, and only evil . . . We wish now also to ask the American people to remember that the Chinese in this country have been for the most part peaceable and industrious . . . We have toiled patiently to build your railroads, to aid in harvesting your fruits and grain, and to reclaim your swamp lands. Our presence and labor on this coast we believe have made possible numerous manufacturing interests which, without us, could not exist on these shores. . . . In view of all these facts we are constrained to ask why this bitter hostility against the few thousands of Chinese in America! Why these severe and barbarous enactments, discriminating against us, in favor of other nationalities.

Other Chinese people resisted the discriminatory laws in other ways. In 1878, a Chinese immigrant named Ho Ah Kow was working in San Francisco. He didn't have many choices about where to live. Most men like him could not afford and were not welcomed in housing outside of the crowded, shared living quarters of Chinatown. Ah Kow probably lived in a cramped boardinghouse with other Chinese workmen. We know Ho Ah Kow's name today because he was one of the Chinese people charged with violating the Cubic Air Ordinance. He was given two choices: Pay a fine of ten dollars or go to the county jail for five days. Ten dollars was a lot of money for a struggling laborer, and Ah Kow was either unable or unwilling to pay. Like so many other Chinese people charged under the Cubic Air Ordinance, Ho Ah Kow was sent to the county jail. There, in a further humiliation, the jailers shaved Ah Kow's hair down to an inch under the Pigtail Ordinance.

A cartoon in the March 2, 1878, edition of the San Francisco Illustrated Wasp, *showing Sheriff Nunan placing Chinese men arrested for violating the "500 cubic foot" law into a county jail space of 100 cubic feet.*

Ho Ah Kow realized that he had been treated unjustly, and he decided to do something about it. He went to the Chinese Consolidated Benevolent Association, often known as the Six Companies, a group of the six most powerful Chinese associations, to ask for their support in making things right. The Six Companies had the knowledge and money to help Ho Ah Kow sue the San Francisco sheriff in federal court. The sheriff was an Irish immigrant named Matthew Nunan. Like many Chinese Americans, Matthew had arrived in California during the Gold Rush and had spent years searching for gold in the mines. Unlike many Chinese Americans, Matthew Nunan had been able to take his earnings from the mines and convert them into wealth, opening a grocery store and a popular brewery and, later in life, founding a bank. Matthew Nunan became sheriff of San Francisco in 1875 and won reelection two years later. During his time as sheriff, he and his deputies oversaw the cutting of countless Chinese men's queues. One of these men was Ho Ah Kow.

With the associations' support, Ho Ah Kow sued Sheriff Nunan. His case made it all the way to a federal appeals court, and Ah Kow successfully proved the harm that this practice had caused him. In 1879, the court ruled that the Pigtail Ordinance was *discriminatory,* an action that targets or causes harm to a group because of their race, gender, religion, or other identities. The court banned the practice of cutting off queues. Queues became less and less common as the 1800s became the 1900s and disappeared almost entirely after the end of the Qing Dynasty in China in 1912.

LAWS LIKE the Cubic Air Ordinance and the Pigtail Ordinance show how some non-Chinese people were uncomfortable with the growing Chinese population. Chinatowns seemed to be popping up across the country, and the existence of these Chinatowns meant that Chinese immigrants were putting down roots in their new country. Many other Americans were not happy about it.

To understand what people were thinking and saying in history, it helps to look at primary source documents that were created at the time. Sometimes, reading prejudiced language and ideas published in the past can feel offensive and hurtful to us today, but seeing the exact language that people used helps to show us how those with power thought about groups they believed were less worthy. And there were probably many people, including those who were the target of the prejudice, who had to read these words and found them offensive or hurtful even then. Keep that in mind when you read the way a publication called the *Annals of San Francisco, 1855* (a book that drew from newspaper reports and firsthand accounts of the early histories of San Francisco, mostly through the lens of white, upper-class, educated, Protestant residents of the city) summarized the racist beliefs that some people held about Chinese immigrants: "The manners and habits of the Chinese are very repugnant to Americans in California. Of different language, blood, religion and character, inferior in most mental and bodily qualities, the Chinaman is looked upon by some as only a little superior to [Black people], and by others as somewhat inferior." The authors argued that Chinese immigrants were experiencing racist treatment both from individuals and through discriminatory laws. Notice, too, how this early description of Chinese Americans directly compares their place in society with Black Americans', a common practice you will encounter many more times throughout this book. Although the authors noted that this discriminatory treatment was not right, it didn't seem to change many people's minds. Anger and fears about the growing Chinese population continued to heat up, and in many places the strong emotions started to boil over.

THE LOS ANGELES CHINATOWN MASSACRE

On October 24, 1871, a group of about five hundred people, mostly white, stormed into Chinatown in Los Angeles, California, and started beating, shooting, and hanging Chinese people. This event, often called the Los Angeles Chinatown Massacre, is one of the many deadly incidents of racial terror in United States history.

It's all said to have begun as a conflict between two rival associations. A Chinese woman was supposed to marry an older merchant from one of the associations. Depending on who you asked, some people said she ran away with a young man from the other association instead. Other people said she was kidnapped by the young man. Either way, the conflict between the two associations intensified into a shoot-out. Police officers were called to the scene, and one of the responding officers, as well as a white civilian named Robert Thompson, were killed in the cross fire.

Robert Thompson was a popular man, and outrage over his and the police officer's deaths quickly spread across the city. About five hundred angry rioters made their way to Chinatown for revenge. The rioters did not care whether the people they attacked had actually been a part of the association shoot-out. The association fight was just one more incident adding to the anger and mistrust they felt about the Chinese community in general. After the deaths of Robert Thompson and the police officer, the rioters were out for blood, and any Chinese person would do. By the next morning, at least eighteen Chinese people had been killed. About 10 percent of Los Angeles's total population had participated in the angry riot, and about 10 percent

A headline in the Indiana Sentinel *from September 9, 1885, reporting the Rock Springs Massacre.*

of the city's Chinese population had lost their lives. Only one of these people is thought to have been part of the original association gunfight.

At first it seemed possible that there might be some sort of justice for the violence. Twenty-five of the rioters were brought in front of a grand jury to decide whether they should be charged with a crime for their role in the killings. Eight men were convicted of manslaughter, but all of their convictions were overturned. In the end, nobody was held accountable for the brutal massacre. Similar killings occurred across the country in places where groups of Chinese Americans lived and worked in close-knit communities. In 1885, in Rock Springs, Wyoming, at least twenty-eight Chinese miners were killed by white miners who blamed the Chinese immigrants for their hardships in making a living. Throughout the United States, Chinatowns were regularly set on fire by angry individuals or groups, hurting people and destroying property. Many people today are not aware of the Chinese communities in cities like Denver and San Jose whose early Chinatowns were destroyed by racist violence.

The violence against Chinese people in the West followed the same strategies of racial terror that were used against Black and Indigenous Americans throughout the country, showing that events like the Los Angeles Chinatown Massacre were not just the acts of some angry, racist individuals but were part of a broader pattern of oppression and violence. This violence was designed to keep Chinese people from trying to expand the idea of who could be an American and to send a strong message that they would never belong. The violence was also designed to keep Chinese people from developing communities and businesses that would compete with white-owned businesses. Racial terror is not only used to punish people who are establishing wealth or advocating for rights, but it is also used to create fear that at any point your property can be destroyed or your life can be taken without consequence. Racial terror is used to stop people from trying to belong in the first place.

In spite of the negative stereotypes, the discriminatory laws, and the threat of violence, the people of America's Chinatowns found ways to resist oppression. After the Los Angeles Chinatown Massacre, the Los Angeles associations raised money to give the victims of the massacre proper funerals. In less than a year they raised eight thousand dollars, a huge amount of money for poor immigrants and a symbol of how the Chinese community worked together to make life a little better for one another. The year after the massacre, almost all of the Chinese laundry owners in Los Angeles refused to pay their business license fees to the city. Some people think this is the earliest example of Chinese American civil disobedience, or peacefully breaking a law that someone feels is wrong to begin with. Civil disobedience is one strategy people use to draw attention to injustices and to advocate for greater civil rights for all people. The business workers who refused to pay their license fees after the Los Angeles Chinatown Massacre were near the beginning of a long legacy of Chinese Americans peacefully standing up for their own civil rights and for justice for all marginalized people.

LET'S THINK ABOUT THIS:

1. What is an "origin story," and why do people care about origin stories? What origin stories do the people in your life tell?

2. What are the conditions that make people leave their families and homes to start a new life, even if there is no guarantee that they will be successful? What would cause you to travel across an ocean alone to try to find your fortune, without any way of easily communicating with the people you left behind?

3. Some of the racist stereotypes about early Chinese Americans, like the perpetual foreigner stereotype and the idea that they carried diseases, continue to exist. Where have you seen these stereotypes, and how do these affect people today? What do you think needs to happen so that harmful stereotypes stop being spread?

CHAPTER 2

RAILROADS

Before highways and passenger cars, airplanes and cross-country trucking, it took a very long time for people or merchandise to travel across the land that is now the United States. It once took six months by wagon just to get from California to Nebraska, and it would have taken much longer to go even farther east. Faster modes of transportation, like the stagecoach, took about twenty-five days to cover the same distance and were too expensive for most travelers or for the mass transportation of goods. Wagons and stagecoaches both relied on horses, which meant additional costs in feeding the animals and additional care to keep them healthy across the long, often difficult journey.

A stagecoach in Yellowstone National Park, Wyoming, in 1913.

The introduction of the railroad changed everything. Steam engine trains suddenly made the vast distance between the West and East Coasts seem not quite so vast any longer. The distance that once took six months or twenty-five days to travel could now be covered in only four days. Because they did not rely on animals, railroads could run day and night. Trains didn't need to stop and rest like horses did. Plus, railroads could carry far more people and items, far more affordably. The railroads made it easier for passengers to get from one place to another and made it easier for goods produced in one part of the country to be sold in another. Some people realized that this new form of transportation could help them make a better living, because they could more easily acquire what they needed or sell what they produced across greater distances. Other people, seeing the economic possibilities of this new mode of transportation, realized that they could become rich through the railroads themselves.

The mid-1800s saw the rise of a new type of wealthy American: the railroad tycoon. You might recognize the last names of men like Cornelius Vanderbilt and Leland Stanford who took their existing wealth and, through expanding and operating railroads, gained even greater fortune and built institutions that would keep their names famous for generations to come. Leland Stanford was one of the first presidents of a railroad company known as the Central Pacific. Leland originally traveled to California during the Gold Rush to seek his fortune. Unlike the Chinese Americans who arrived for the Gold Rush, however, Leland Stanford came from a relatively wealthy, white, and established family from New York. He had already been a practicing lawyer and elected official before he showed up in California. His time in California would bring him even greater wealth and power.

In the mid-1800s, the U.S. Congress started paying people to form companies that would build a railroad to connect the East and West Coasts—widely known as the Transcontinental Railroad. Leland Stanford and three other businessmen formed the Central Pacific Railroad to construct its westernmost portion.

A newspaper illustration from 1875 showing the Big Four of the Central Pacific Railroad.

The Central Pacific Railroad was in charge of building the stretch of the Transcontinental Railroad that would connect the seven hundred miles between Sacramento, California, and Promontory, Utah. The track would have to cross the often steep and treacherous Sierra Nevada Mountains, and they needed to find people to complete this work within the timeline set by the government. Stanford and his colleagues, a group of wealthy white men often called the "Big Four," knew a thing or two about the economic conditions in California at the time. Most of them first operated as merchants and shopkeepers when they'd arrived in the state, serving miners and others with greater financial struggles than their own. When they needed to find cheap workers to construct their new railroad, they knew exactly where to turn.

ONE OF THE MOST COMMON stories that people today hear about Chinese Americans is that many of them came to the United States to build the railroads. In the 1860s, between fifteen thousand and twenty thousand people of Chinese descent helped to build the Transcontinental Railroad. Some of these Chinese Americans had already been living in Chinatowns on the West Coast, while others came from China for the sole purpose of working on the railroad. Railroad work was one of the few jobs available for people of Chinese descent, but even the railroad industry did not originally intend to employ Chinese laborers.

In 1865, the Big Four's Central Pacific Railroad put out a job advertisement to find workers to help build their new line. Historical records suggest that they initially expected to hire a white workforce. Most of the white workers they planned to recruit would have been of Irish descent who, like the Chinese, were often fleeing poverty and hunger in their homeland. Irish workers also faced discrimination and poor treatment in the United States, and many struggled to find work. The Big Four thought it would be pretty easy to find enough Irish and other poor white workers who would be willing to build their railroad. Instead, the physically demanding reality of a railroad job did not appeal to most of these potential white workers. Irish Americans faced real discrimination in their new country and had to take on unpleasant, difficult labor, and yet many were able to find better options than working on the railroad, one of the most punishing jobs of all. Only a few hundred Irish people responded to the Central Pacific's job advertisement.

The owners of the Central Pacific Railroad needed to find workers quickly, so a man named Charles Crocker, one of Leland Stanford's colleagues in the Big Four, suggested that they try to hire Chinese workers instead. At first, the other people in charge of the railroad were unhappy with this idea. Some people repeated racist beliefs about Chinese people as untrustworthy and disease-ridden. Others believed that Chinese workers wouldn't be strong enough to do the physical work required to lay new tracks. However, the Big Four felt they did not have a choice. Their need to find workers who could finish the project on time outweighed their prejudice against Chinese people. In the end, about 80 or 90 percent of Central Pacific Railroad workers were Chinese.

They might have found employment, but these Chinese American workers did not escape prejudice

A camp of Chinese workers in Nevada, building the first transcontinental railroad in 1890.

and discrimination. The people in charge of the railroad paid Chinese people less than the smaller group of white people who were hired to work on the same lines. White workers were sometimes allowed to sleep in train cars, but Chinese workers typically had to live in tents or shacks that were much more exposed to the elements. Working conditions were rough. There were no cranes or bulldozers, power drills or jackhammers. Workers had to do most of the work by hand. Many railroad workers spent whole days shoveling rocks, up to twenty pounds at a time, over four hundred times a day. Not only was the work exhausting, but it was also dangerous. The temperatures in the mountains could be well below freezing, and workers were sometimes killed by avalanches and rockslides. The winter of 1867 brought forty-four snowstorms, and miners had to dig passages through the snow in order to get around. The workers were cold, exhausted, and often hungry. They relied on the railroad company in order to eat. In fact, the Chinese workers were required to give some of the low wages they earned from the Central Pacific right back to the company to pay for their food.

On top of all the hardships that the Big Four and the other overseers of the railroad imposed on the workers, there was another, equally unforgiving force they had to contend with: the Sierra Nevada Mountains.

THE RAILROAD NEEDED to cross the Sierra Nevada Mountains, and some parts would need to reach elevations of about seven thousand feet above sea level. The Big Four and their head engineers thought it would be too expensive and complicated to only go over the top of the mountains. Instead, they decided that in some places they would have to dig through them. Building tunnels through the mountains was an especially arduous and dangerous process.

Imagine standing in front of a giant, solid

mountain and being told that you have to make a hole through the center of it. You can only use hand tools and some weak explosives. You have to keep working in all kinds of weather, including blizzards, without much rest and without a comfortable place to sleep. And you have to do all of this thousands of miles away from your family, with almost no way to contact them. This was the task in front of the Chinese railroad workers.

In spite of all of these challenges, the Chinese workers proved to be quite skillful at building tunnels. They would begin by chipping small holes into the solid granite using hammers and chisels. Then they would pack an explosive into the holes. The workers would light the explosive and run as quickly as they could back toward the mouth of the tunnel to avoid getting hurt in the explosion. When the dust settled, they would go back to the site of the explosion to clear away the rock that had been blasted into smaller chunks from the solid granite. Using baskets, carts, and sometimes just their bare hands, the workers would haul these pieces of rock back out of the tunnel until it was clear enough to start the whole process all over again. As you can imagine, many people were injured or even lost their lives in this process. Workers had to be alert, clever, and strong to undertake their dangerous work.

The method workers used to build tunnels for the Central Pacific Railroad.

The most difficult tunnel to construct was the Summit Tunnel, which required digging through 1,659 feet (or almost one-third of a mile) of solid granite. At one point between 1866 and 1867, about eight thousand Chinese railroad workers worked in three shifts that rotated endlessly throughout the days and nights. They slowly chipped away at the granite from four directions: workers headed toward the center of the tunnel from both outside ends, and workers headed from the center toward the outside in both directions. At first they used blasting powder, also known as black powder, to help slowly clear the way. Using this method, the tunnel grew at a pace of fourteen inches per day. Eventually, railroad engineers made a switch to nitroglycerin, a stronger explosive. At the new rate of twenty-two inches per day, the pace of excavation increased slightly. To connect the railroad through the new tunnel, workers also laid down tracks and rails, which they secured by hammering giant iron spikes into the hard earth and stone.

Given the challenges and dangers of the work and the slow pace of manual labor, the engineers who designed the Summit Tunnel thought that it would take three years to complete, but it was completed in sixteen months—less than half of the prediction. This faster rate was largely connected to two important details about the Chinese railroad workers. First, China has a long history of complex engineering. Even Charles Crocker of the Big Four said, "They built the Great Wall of China, didn't they?" Gunpowder was also invented in China, and the Summit Tunnel would never have been completed in time without a complex understanding of explosives. Although most Chinese immigrants would not have had advanced knowledge of engineering and gunpowder, a few would have. Many historians believe that these contributions of Chinese knowledge helped with the successful construction of the railroad. In an impressive display of speed and skill, one crew of many Chinese men and eight Irish men was able to lay ten miles of railroad track in a single day, a record that still stands today.

Another, and sadder, reason for the fast completion rate was that the railroad owners and many others viewed Chinese workers as cheap and replaceable. Here is how the record ten-mile track was described in a publication from 1928:

FIFTY-NINE years ago a squad of eight Irishmen and a small army of Chinese coolies made a record in track laying that has never been equalled. In one day, on April 28, 1869, these men, fired with the enthusiasm of the greatest railroad construction race in the history of the world, laid ten miles and fifty-six feet of track in a little less than twelve hours to bring the railhead of the Central Pacific three and one-half miles from Promontory, Utah, where connection was made a few days later with the Union Pacific to form the first transcontinental railroad.

The names of the Irish rail handlers have been passed down through the years. Their super-human

achievement will be remembered as long as there is
railroad history.

So, too, will that day's work of "John China-
man" be recalled as the most stirring event in the
building of the railroad.

In this publication, you can see the difference in the way that Chinese workers and Irish workers were thought about and treated. The author writes that the eight Irish workers will be honored, and that their individual names will live in history. On the other hand, the author calls Chinese workers "coolies"—a slur for Chinese peasants. Either nobody was quite sure of how many Chinese workers were really there, or the author did not bother to report that informa tion. All the Chinese workers are referred to as a single being, rather than given individual recognition. Instead, the Chinese workers' names are reduced to another stereotype: "John Chinaman."

The Chinese workers were forced by their overseers and the railroad owners to work with little care for their health or safety, because if one worker got injured or was killed, the owners of the railroad could easily hire another one. Their individual lives were seen as unimportant. As a result, there are few existing records that allow people today to know the exact names and stories of the Chinese people who worked on the railroad, or what happened to them. What we do know is that about twelve hundred people with Chinese ancestry died building the Transcontinental Railroad. Some of these people considered China to be their home, while others were born in the United States and considered themselves both Chinese and American. About one thousand of the people who died working on the railroads asked to have their bodies sent back to China after death. Maybe they felt like China was their true home, or maybe they were

A funeral procession of Chinese railroad workers near Dutch Flat, California.

made to feel like they didn't belong in their new land. One thing is clear: The people in charge of the railroads must not have minded all the death, because they continued to force workers to maintain their very fast pace in spite of the danger.

Today, it is widely agreed that Chinese people were essential to the completion of the Transcontinental Railroad. But when the Central Pacific Railroad was first completed, the Big Four and other important leaders of the railroad largely overlooked all that the Chinese workers had given to the company—including their knowledge, hard work, and sometimes their lives. In 1869, the Central Pacific Railroad finally met up with the Union Pacific Railroad, meaning that the first transcontinental railroad was completed. A famous photograph was taken to celebrate the occasion. You might even recognize it from your textbooks at school. The photo shows a large group of men standing in front of two trains, and the group includes leaders, engineers, and manual laborers of both railroads. Only two of the men in the photograph are Chinese. One of them has his back to the camera. The people who did most of the difficult, deadly work to reach this celebration are almost entirely missing from the picture.

The famous photo of the joining of the Union Pacific and Central Pacific Railroads, taken by Andrew J. Russell in Promontory, Utah, on May 10, 1869.

RESISTANCE ON THE RAILROADS

Chinese workers may have contributed their skill and labor to help achieve the completion of the Transcontinental Railroad, but that doesn't mean that they happily accepted the harsh treatment and terrible working conditions. The Chinese workers were aware of the unfair treatment they received compared to the smaller group of white, mostly Irish people working for the same railroad company. Sometimes, the Chinese workers were paid half of what the white workers were paid for the same work. And unlike most white workers, Chinese workers had to pay for their own food, lodging, and tools. In 1867, a group of Chinese workers decided they were sick of it. They wanted better pay, shorter hours, and safer working conditions, and they were not going to build another inch of railroad until they got it. Up and down the line, Chinese workers organized a strike to peacefully protest for their collective rights.

Can you imagine how complicated it must have been to organize this strike? The workers were spread out across long stretches of track, and they did not have regular breaks to go visit with one another across the various camps. The terrain was difficult to travel, and workers were already exhausted from their daily tasks. The planning would have to happen in secret, because if the owners of the railroad learned that the workers were planning to strike, they would immediately shut it down. Unlike today, there were no cell phones or social media to communicate plans. Instead, the strike must have been planned over many different conversations in various small groups over a period of time. Many of the workers were probably scared about the consequences of going on strike, and others would have had to convince them to join in the collective demand for better treatment. Only by everyone joining together in a show of solidarity would the workers have enough power to stand up to the Big Four and their other bosses. Through networking, persuasion, and careful planning, the workers were finally ready to strike. On June 25, 1867, thousands of workers went to their camps, laid down their tools, and sat down. They had just begun what has been called the largest workers' strike of the era.

When he learned of the strike, Charles Crocker was impressed by the Chinese workers' sense of community and their ability to work together. He was also very angry and a little bit scared. There were far more Chinese people than white people working along the line, and Charles worried that giving in to the demands of the strike would give too much power to the Chinese workers. With every day that went by,

Charles and the other bosses were losing money. The Chinese workers knew that the government paid the railroad company for every mile laid, so the faster they worked the richer the men like Charles Crocker became. The Chinese laborers figured that stopping work entirely would get the attention of their bosses. And it did. The bosses were frantic and tried to get people back to work as quickly as possible. Instead of listening to the workers' demands, the bosses used intimidation to try to end the strike. They cut off food to the striking workers and threatened to withhold their pay. In spite of these threats, the Chinese laborers held strong in their beliefs that they deserved better treatment. The strike continued.

The men of the Big Four became more and more desperate. Two of them, Charles Crocker and a man named Mark Hopkins, advocated for a very different solution. Instead of forcing the Chinese people to return to work, maybe they could forget about these men and find an entirely new source of cheap labor. It was 1869, just four years after the end of the Civil War. Millions of formerly enslaved Black Americans were now, in theory, free to choose their own work. However, just because slavery was illegal doesn't mean that anti-Black racism had ended. Most Black Americans had been denied the resources, like land and money, to start their own businesses or comfortably sustain their own families. And yet, many white people did not want to employ and fairly pay free Black Americans, either.

Many Black Americans were struggling to find work, and Charles Crocker and Mark Hopkins saw an opportunity. In a strategy that has been used by people in power throughout history, the bosses of the Central Pacific Railroad thought they could use one group of marginalized people—free Black Americans—to motivate or replace another group of marginalized people—the poorly treated and over-worked Chinese Americans. This was the same tactic that was used when the Central Pacific Railroad first began and not enough poor Irish people would take on the new jobs. Mark Hopkins himself explicitly described the plan to use this *divide and conquer* strategy to break the strike, saying, "A [Black] labor force would tend to keep the Chinese steady, as the Chinese have kept the Irishmen quiet." The Big Four never enacted this proposed strategy, however, and still the strike continued.

Charles Crocker told the Chinese workers that he was never going to give in to their demands for better pay or easier hours. Instead, he charged a fine to all the workers for the days that they had missed. This might seem harsh on its own, but he also said that he would charge them even more if they did not return to work immediately. He would not pay them for the entire month of June. Many of the starving workers felt like they had no choice. After eight days, the most powerful force in the standoff turned out to be hunger. The workers were so hungry, and the only way that they could afford or access food was through the railroad company. Most of the workers reluctantly picked up their tools and headed back to their labor. Still, some of the workers continued to resist. Charles threatened to send men with guns up into the mountains to force these last holdouts to end their strike. With their physical safety under threat, the remaining strikers went back to work.

Although some might call the strike a failure, it was a powerful demonstration of organizing and solidarity. The Chinese workers had done the difficult work of organizing a large, diverse group of people around a common belief: the idea that they deserved fair treatment and a living wage, and that their health and lives mattered.

The principles that the Chinese workers were standing up for when they went on strike from the Central Pacific Railroad are the same principles that have motivated other labor movements throughout U.S. history. Today, when you hear about workers going on strike, see if you notice any similarities between what they say they are experiencing and what the Chinese railroad workers experienced. When people go on strike, they often explain that it is because of low pay, dangerous working conditions, and a feeling that the people above them care more about making money than about the people who do the most physically demanding work. Just like the Chinese railroad workers in 1869, many workers in the United States continue to organize to demand better treatment for all people. For another example of Chinese Americans who organized for workers' rights, look up the 1982 Garment Workers' Strike, when nearly twenty thousand workers, mostly Chinese American women, joined together in New York City to gain better pay and working conditions.

● ● ●

The North Adams Strike of 1870

Chinese American workers have found themselves at different ends of labor strikes. While the Chinese railroad workers went on strike in solidarity, other Chinese workers were used as part of divide and conquer tactics to break other strikes.

In 1870, workers at a shoe factory in North Adams, Massachusetts, went on strike. These workers were mostly white, from Irish or Canadian backgrounds. Some were Civil War veterans. Like the Chinese railroad workers, the shoe factory workers were demanding better pay and treatment. The owners of the factory did not want to give in to these demands, so they turned to divide and conquer instead. The factory manager fired all the Irish workers and replaced them with Chinese laborers who would take on the same jobs for lower wages. This ended up hurting all of the workers: the Irish, Canadian, and veteran workers, who had lost their income and employment, and the Chinese workers, who were now subjected to the poor working conditions and even lower pay than before. The only people who benefited were the factory owners.

Unfortunately, divide and conquer worked in this instance. The Irish and Chinese workers did not realize they had been used against each other, and tensions between the groups grew. The story of the North Adams strike spread across the country and was used to stoke fears about Chinese people coming to steal jobs from white American workers. This incident helped pave the way for later laws restricting Chinese immigration, which you can read about in Chapter 5.

LET'S THINK ABOUT THIS:

1. The associations, Ho Ah Kow, the railroad workers, and the other people you have read about so far used different strategies to advocate for their individual and collective rights. What lessons can we learn from these examples to advocate for more people's rights today?

2. In the 1928 article about the famous ten-mile track, the Irish workers and the Chinese workers are described in very different ways. Why do you think that is? How would these differences affect the way someone reading this article would think or feel about the two groups?

3 The most common story about Chinese Americans that is taught in schools is that they helped to build the railroads. Which parts of this story were familiar to you already, and which parts were new? Why do you think some parts of this story are taught more often than others?

CHAPTER 3

HARD WORK

Picture a highway on which all the vehicles are going in one direction. There is one place to get on the highway at its beginning, and there is one destination that all the cars are headed toward at its end. This is how many people think about immigration. They imagine that all the people start in one place and move in the same direction, at basically the same rate, toward the other place. Sometimes, the story of Chinese Americans is told in this simplistic way. The story that most people learn about Chinese Americans is that Chinese people all left the same region in China and came to build railroads in California. But, just like highways don't really work this way, immigration doesn't work this way either.

Instead, people join the highway in lots of different places, for lots of different reasons. Some move quickly; some move slowly. Some vehicles have just one driver; others are full of passengers. Sometimes people leave the highway for a while, or decide to go back to their starting point, or head off to another location entirely.

As you already know, many early Chinese Americans traveled to the United States for reasons besides the railroad, like to mine for gold or to work in a Chinatown. You also know that many of these early Chinese Americans felt more of a connection to China than to the U.S., and many were buried in China after their deaths. So you can probably already guess that, as more Chinese people started to move back and forth between China and the United States, the story becomes even more complicated. The first Chinatowns were mostly clustered around the gold mines of Northern California, but the railroad opened up new employment opportunities. Small Chinatowns sprung up around coal mines that employed Chinese workers. Some went as far east as New York City, which today has the highest concentration of Chinese people in the United States. Across the country, Chinese people found work in jobs as diverse as mining, field labor, domestic servitude, cooking, and more.

Domestic Servitude

Chinese Americans who worked in the homes of white families were domestic servants. Both men and women held these jobs, though in the 1800s there were far more Chinese American men in the United States than women. As a result, Chinese domestic servants were often referred to by the derogatory term "houseboy." These men cooked, cleaned, did laundry, took care of children and animals, ran errands, and did anything else their employers asked of them. Some examples from pop culture are the character Hop Sing from the old Western TV show *Bonanza* and the character Lee from John Steinbeck's *East of Eden.*

LAUNDRY

One industry with a long Chinese American history is laundry. Yes, you read that right: laundry. Many Chinese American families were able to establish themselves and build their futures upon this humble chore.

By the mid-1800s, some people, mostly white, had managed to get rich in the Gold Rush. With more money to spend, these people started buying nicer clothes to wear, and they needed someone to properly clean and care for these clothes. Most of these newly well-off people were men who had traveled alone to California, and most of these men felt like they were now too good to do laundry, or they simply didn't know how to. They often thought of laundry as a "woman's job," and therefore, beneath them. Without many other options, it became pretty common for people to ship their laundry all the way to Hong Kong to be cleaned. This took nearly four months and cost about twelve dollars for a dozen shirts, which is equal to about four hundred dollars today. Still, this was way cheaper than the alternative, to send the clothes back to the East Coast of the United States to be cleaned. Remember, the Transcontinental Railroad wasn't finished yet, so the laundry would have had to go by boat all the way around the continent or over land on a wagon. Hong Kong was the best option for people with the money to spend on laundry, and so the shipment of clothing back and forth across the Pacific Ocean became another link between the coasts of the United States and China, another lane on the highway connecting Chinese Americans between their two lands.

In the middle of the Pacific Ocean, and closer to San Francisco than to Hong Kong, you will find the islands of Hawai'i. By the mid-1800s, Hawai'i had become a stopover for people and goods as they went back and forth between China and the West Coast of the continental United States. The rich people who had been shipping their laundry to Hong Kong now had a closer, more affordable option. Instead of spending twelve dollars to have a dozen shirts washed in Hong Kong, they could spend eight dollars to have a dozen shirts washed in Honolulu.

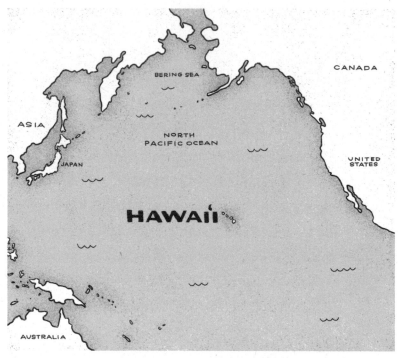

A map showing the position of Hawai'i between Asia and North America.

Pretty soon, some Chinese people in California realized that they might be able to make a good living by starting laundry businesses in the continental United States itself. There were few options for Chinese Americans who did not want to work in the mines or do other types of manual labor. Remember, newspapers and other sources regularly repeated racist stereotypes about Chinese people during this time, and people who ran cities and states with large Chinese populations passed laws like the Cubic Air Ordinance that targeted Chinese people because of these stereotypes. Many white people and white-owned businesses in these places did not want to hire Chinese people, except as outdoor laborers or as domestic servants. Language was also an issue, and jobs that required fluent reading, writing, or speaking in English were out of reach for many Chinese immigrants. Most Chinese Americans would probably have preferred to create their own businesses, but this, too, was difficult. To open a store that sells food or goods, you first need to have enough money to buy the things that you will eventually try to sell, and few Chinese Americans had this sort of starting money.

Laundry was a solution that addressed all of these problems. Very few white people wanted to own or operate laundries, so the white community would not feel threatened by Chinese people opening laundries. Doing laundry does not require speaking fluent English. In fact, some Chinese laundry owners drew images of different-sized coins that they could point at to demonstrate the price of their services, so that they did not have to talk to customers in English or read the money that was passed back and forth. And it does not require much starting money to begin a laundry business: all you need is soap, a bucket or barrel, a board to scrub the clothes on, and an iron. While many white Americans of this time period would have considered laundry to be a low-status job, many early Chinese Americans saw an opportunity instead.

In 1851, a man named Wah Lee reportedly opened the first Chinese-owned laundry in the United States. He charged five dollars to clean a dozen shirts, good earnings for a Chinese immigrant in San Francisco. By opening his laundry business, Wah Lee had ended the need for wealthy Californians to ship laundry as far as Honolulu and Hong Kong when it could be done faster and cheaper right at home. Pretty quickly, other Chinese Americans caught on to the new opportunity and opened their own laundries. This was difficult work, and many laundry workers spent up to sixteen hours a day sweating over vats of hot water, bending their backs over a washboard and iron, and handling dirty items like other people's used underwear and handkerchiefs. It might sound unpleasant. It probably was unpleasant! But it was also probably a relief after the dangers and blatant racism of the mines and railroads. Owning or working in a laundry meant not having to fight with other people over mining claims or having to work for a harsh railroad overseer. For many Chinese Americans, owning or working in a laundry meant *autonomy*, the freedom to make one's own decisions.

Laundry work was not easy, but to many Chinese Americans it represented a chance at the "American Dream." By the time the 1800s were turning into the 1900s, the laundry industry was almost entirely associated with Chinese people. These Chinese-run laundries, sometimes called Chinese hand laundries, spread from coast to coast. At the height of the industry, there were more than five thousand Chinese-run laundry businesses around New York City alone! Some statistics suggest that by 1900, one in every four Chinese men in the United States worked in the laundry industry. Many Chinese Americans today can still recall memories of growing up in their family's laundry, helping to press and fold, and how the piles of clothes represented their family's hard work, hopes for the future, and belief that they would be able to survive.

SUGAR

While laundries were a central industry for Chinese Americans in towns and cities, difficult physical labor outdoors continued to be the work for many others. Their work in mines provided coal that fueled the same railroads they had helped to build. Their work as servants often included tending to property and livestock for their employers. They also worked in fields, planting and harvesting crops that could be used as food, clothing, and other commodities to be bought and sold. One place where Chinese people labored outside was on the tropical, volcanic soil of the Hawaiian Islands. While for some people (and their laundry!) Hawai'i was seen as a stopover between China and the U.S., for others Hawai'i was a destination in and of itself.

This book focuses on the experiences of Chinese Americans, but to understand their experiences in Hawai'i in the mid-1800s we have to first understand that this was a period of significant political change in the islands. In 1850, Hawai'i was still an independent kingdom, ruled by King Kamehameha the Third. The Hawaiian Kingdom had been established in 1795 when the islands were unified under the power of Kamehameha the Great. The Hawaiian

Kingdom was recognized as an independent nation by many European countries, and trade was common between the islands, Europe, and the United States. Even so, these connections were very new. The first European to arrive in the Hawaiian Islands was a British navy captain named James Cook, and he did not arrive until the late 1700s. Today, many people know James as a great explorer, but the truth is that his explorations also led him to be a violent colonizer. James Cook was killed in 1779 while attempting to kidnap a Hawaiian chief. In the decades that followed, white Europeans and Americans continued to exert influence and control over the islands, often with violent repercussions.

One of the reasons that white Europeans and Americans wanted control over the islands was the perfect growing conditions for sugarcane. Sugar is wildly popular today, and the same was true when it started becoming more readily available in the 1800s. There is an almost endless demand for sugar, and so a fortune can be made by growing, processing, and selling it. The techniques to grow, harvest, and process sugar had been honed by enslaved Black and Indigenous people working without pay on white-owned plantations in the Caribbean and the southern United States. White people established sugar plantations in Hawaiʻi in the 1830s, and they needed people to work in the fields. At first, they turned to Kānaka Maoli, or Native Hawaiians, who understandably hated doing the backbreaking, low-wage work for these foreign businessmen. The first recorded strike in Hawai'i occurred in 1841, with Native Hawaiians walking off their plantation jobs. Like the Chinese railroad workers' strike, this strike was not ultimately successful, but it rattled the white plantation owners. They realized that there would not be enough Native Hawaiian people who were able or willing to work to meet the demand for sugar, and so they looked for other sources of cheap labor.

Like the railroad tycoons of California, the sugar plantation owners of Hawai'i thought that Chinese people would be a cheap, plentiful, and replaceable source of alternative labor. In 1850, a white American man named William Little Lee was the Chief Justice of the Supreme Court of the Kingdom of Hawai'i. He wrote and helped enact a law called the Masters and Servants Act, which aimed to cheaply import human laborers to work in the fields. In 1852, 192 Chinese contract workers were brought to Hawai'i under this act to work on sugarcane plantations. These first workers agreed to a five-year contract in which they would be given food, lodging, and three dollars a month.

If the name "Masters and Servants Act" reminds you of systems of slavery, it's because the system of contract labor had many similarities to enslavement. One of the key differences was that, unlike the hereditary enslavement of Black Americans in the continental United States, contracts were not passed from parents to their children. In other words, *chattel slavery,* the enslaving and owning of human beings and their offspring as property, did not exist in Hawai'i like it had for enslaved Black Americans in the continental U.S. Even so, the system of contract labor was brutal. The act allowed for workers (the "servants") to be brought to Hawai'i under contract, but it gave their employers (the "masters") the power to decide if and how they would uphold their end of the contract. There are many reports of employers changing or extending contracts without notifying their workers, or of imprisoning or beating workers without much chance for the workers to do anything about it.

As more people across the world got a taste for sugar, demand only continued to increase. And so, the demand for people who could cultivate, harvest, and process sugar also continued to increase. Then, during the American Civil War, the supply of sugar from the southern United States was significantly cut. Black Americans were self-emancipating, leaving their work in the sugarcane fields for freedom or for service in the Union Army. Military blockades limited the transportation of goods. In both the North and South, energy was diverted to producing supplies that would support the war effort. With all of this turmoil, Hawai'i was now the main provider of sugar. In the four decades following the passage of the Masters and Servants Act, almost 50,000 more Chinese people followed the first 192 contract laborers to Hawai'i. Their days involved ten or more hours of bending over to pull up weeds or chop sugarcane in the stifling tropical heat, typically with only one day of rest per week. Plantation workers might be whipped by their white overseers for standing up to stretch in the fields, and they might be put in jail for trying to leave the plantation before their multiyear contract was over.

The racist stereotypes of California's Chinatowns also persisted in the plantations of Hawai'i. The Center for Labor Education and Research at the University of Hawai'i, West O'ahu provides an example of this kind of thinking. They summarize the positive and negative stereotypes held about Chinese people at the time by writing, "When the Chinese laborer was needed he was praised as quiet, skillful, obedient, patient and quick to learn. When he left the plantation and entered the open labor market, or went into business, he was condemned as a murderer, cutthroat, thief, selfish and cunning."

The last sentence highlights the common stereotype of Chinese people as sneaky and violent. When Chinese railroad workers went on strike, some people described their actions as plotting and planning in the shadows. When Chinese associations stood together to raise money against an unjust law, some people thought they were behaving like selfish cheats. Political cartoons depicting Chinese people as murderers, thieves, and sea pirates were common, and most Americans would have recognized these as common ideas about Chinese Americans, whether they believed them or not. Even many famous Americans that we still celebrate today held these prejudiced ideas. The author Samuel Clemens, whom you might know better as Mark Twain, visited the sugar plantations of Hawai'i and wrote letters that were published in the *Sacramento Daily Union* back in the United States. In 1866, a line from one of his letters summarizes the common stereotype of Chinese workers as strong and efficient, yet somehow evil and dangerous: "Their Former trade of cutting throats on the China seas has made them uncommonly handy at cutting cane." In Hawai'i, like in the continental United States, these racist stereotypes led to racist laws. In 1892, worried that the growing Chinese population would eventually take power away from white people, the planters passed a law saying that Chinese people were only allowed to work in fields and in rice or sugar mills. Unlike in the United States, they would not have the option to open grocery stores or laundries as ways to seek their independence.

The old strategy of divide and conquer was also alive and well on the sugarcane plantations. While most of the early contract laborers were Chinese, they were soon joined by Filipino workers, Portuguese workers, and others. The largest group of imported contract workers were Japanese. Some Native Hawaiians also continued to work on the plantations. Plantation owners paid laborers different wages and gave them different privileges depending on their race, gender, and ethnic backgrounds. Only white workers were allowed to hold positions of authority, like being a plantation overseer. When one group tried to demand better pay or treatment, plantation owners would use the other groups to prevent labor stoppages. By actively creating systems that would make it difficult or undesirable for workers from different backgrounds to work together, the plantation owners were able to keep all of their workers in a position of servitude.

In another similarity between the railroads and

the plantations, most of the economic power in Hawai'i starting in the mid-1800s was controlled by a small group of sugar companies known as the "Big Five." The men who ran these companies made the start of their fortune in sugar, but quickly expanded to other crops and to industries that were related to buying and selling these crops, such as sugar refineries or shipping and banking. The Big Five and their interests wanted to maintain and grow their power.

In 1893, Queen Lili'uokalani ruled over the Kingdom of Hawai'i. A group known as the Committee of Safety led a coup to overthrow the Kingdom. The committee was mostly made up of white Americans with connections to the Big Five and to Christian missionaries. While the Committee of Safety established a new independent nation known as the Republic of Hawai'i, their main goal was to eventually have Hawai'i become a part of the United States, against the will of the queen and her people. The Big Five heavily advocated for this *annexation* of Hawai'i, or the forceful takeover of one place's territory by another. In 1900, the islands became a territory of the United States. In less than one hundred fifty years since first contact with Europeans, the Hawaiian Islands were no longer controlled by the Native peoples who had lived there for generations.

The annexation of Hawai'i brought even more

power and wealth to the top people in the Big Five, while costs and living conditions became increasingly difficult for others. Even though the Big Five were private companies, they held immense political as well as economic power. By 1900, wages for planta-tion laborers had barely changed since the very first contracts. Workers could expect to earn about fifteen dollars a month. In just a few years, Hawai'i had gone from an independent kingdom, led by a proud line of Native monarchs, to a land that was technically controlled by the United States but was, in practice, largely controlled by the interests of a handful of rich and powerful private companies. Queen Lili'uokalani strongly opposed the annexation, and spent many years trying to retain the rights of Kānaka Maoli people. She established organizations that would continue to support her people for generations. The movement to regain Hawaiian sovereignty continues to this day.

As always, however, wherever there are stories of division and oppression there are also stories of soli-darity and resistance. With the fall of the Hawaiian Kingdom, the Masters and Servants Act no longer had power. Many people, freed from their contracts, left Hawai'i and headed back to their homelands or to the mainland United States to find work in a new place. In 1900, the year that Hawai'i became a U.S. territory, there were twenty-five recorded strikes on the islands. Organizing actions continued through the early years of the 1900s. Many of these strikes were organized by Japanese workers, who by this time had become the largest ethnic group working on the plantations. In response, plantation owners doubled down on their divide and conquer strategies. Thinking about humans as commodities rather than people, plantation owners brought in monthly shipments of Puerto Rican workers to prevent any one group—and Japanese people in particular—from maintaining a majority. Later, plantation owners started bringing in larger numbers of workers from the Philippines for the same purpose. Owners increased wages for workers from some groups and not others, threatening any group that organized a strike that they would never see wage increases if they continued to "cause trouble."

But pretty quickly, these diverse groups of low-paid laborers realized what their employers were doing. The divide and conquer tactics backfired. Plantation workers continued to strike and organize, first forming collective power with others from the same country of origin, and eventually across different ethnic groups. The workers realized that they would be more successful together than apart. In 1920, they formed the Hawaii Laborers' Association, the first multi-ethnic labor union on the islands. This new union included Japanese, Chinese, Filipino, Portuguese, and Spanish workers, and it inspired other diverse coalitions to join in solidarity in other industries on the islands. Workers in Hawai'i continued to struggle for their rights throughout the twentieth century, and many still do so today. Over time, these groups also began to intermix in settings outside of work. Many of the Chinese Americans who were brought to Hawai'i as laborers eventually started families with immigrants from other ethnic backgrounds or with Native Hawaiians.

Oftentimes when we talk about cultures coming together, we talk about the blending of foods. Food is part of all of our lives, and food traditions matter to most people. Today, alongside the traditional dishes that Hawaiian people have prepared and eaten for centuries, another form of Hawaiian cuisine has become popular. This food tradition consists of a blend of ingredients and techniques from all over the world, brought to the islands by people who—in spite of all the efforts to divide them—forged connections and solidarity across their differences. This blending of cuisines is often referred to as "plantation food," a nod to the harsh industry that brought these people to the same place, and the experiences of collective struggle that brought them together.

Another important legacy of the solidarity that was forged by many workers on Hawaiian plantations is the formation of multiethnic coalitions that continue to seek collective power today. When you hear terms like Asian Pacific American (APA) or Asian American Pacific Islander (AAPI), think of Hawai'i and the coalitions of people from various parts of Asia as well as the Native Hawaiians who have persisted for decades in trying to form stronger connections across their differences. These coalitions have not always been easy to maintain. Asian Americans in Hawai'i have experienced racism and prejudice and have perpetuated racism and prejudice against others, particularly Native Hawaiians. Solidarity across groups can be difficult, because different groups have different needs. Solidarity requires understanding that we can be different and still work together. Solidarity also requires knowing how to listen to the people and groups that are being most affected by racism and by strategies like divide and conquer. The workers of Hawai'i knew too well that being divided against each other makes all of us weaker.

COTTON

Before this book moves too far into the 1900s, there is another important story of labor to tell. We shift our attention to another place that you might not associate with Chinese people: the Deep South. Chinese Americans found themselves in clustered communities across this region, and our story zooms in on one of these. We turn now to the fertile land known as the Mississippi Delta.

By the late 1800s, the United States government had claimed the lands that spread from the Atlantic Ocean to the Pacific Ocean. The period that is sometimes called "Westward Expansion," which included the U.S. purchase, invasion, and annexation of Indigenous lands, had ended. The railroads were the main way that people and goods traveled from east to west. From north to south, however, travel didn't only happen over land. It happened on the water: the Mississippi River.

The Mississippi is one of the largest rivers in the world. It runs from Lake Itasca in Minnesota all the way to the Gulf of Mexico. From the Gulf, goods can be shipped to be sold all over the world, and goods from other places can be brought in. By the 1800s, the Mississippi River had become an important hub for transportation and trade, but it has represented so much more in the imagination of the United States. The Mississippi River flows through American music, American art, and American literature, showing up in countless songs and stories, paintings and poems. To some, the river represents freedom and opportunity—the best of what it means to be American. To others, the river is a symbol of deep pain—the embodiment of some of the worst aspects of America's story. Good and bad, these waters have become a symbol of the

United States, and people across the world have heard of the Mississippi River.

Sold Down the River

The Mississippi River lives on in our idioms as well. Have you ever heard the expression "to be sold down the river"? The phrase means to be betrayed, but its origins are even more brutal than that. Enslaved people who were sold to plantations farther south, or farther "down the river," faced a terrible fate. Southern plantations had a reputation for being the most violent, and the enslaved people who were separated from their families to be sent farther south had almost no chance of ever seeing their loved ones again.

The Mississippi River also flows through American history. It was the water that gave life to great Native civilizations of the time before white people came to the land. Among these Mississippian civilizations were the Cahokia people, who built large earthen mounds up and down the river. Their cities and complex societies were larger than many European cities of the same time period. Native people today continue to live up and down the river, including Anishinaabe people of the Upper Midwest and Choctaw people of the Deep South. But perhaps the time period that is most associated with the Mississippi River is the decades before and after the American Civil War. The Mississippi River was central to the industry that had made the United States not only a young nation but a rich and powerful one: cotton. And the Mississippi River was central to the brutal institution that allowed for cotton to become king: American chattel slavery.

The Mississippi River does not flow in a straight line, but rather it winds like a snake, often changing direction and creating dramatic S-shapes as it flows toward the sea. Before the invention of levees, or structures that stop flooding and control the movement of water, this snake regularly changed shape and position, and the river never looked quite the same as it had the previous year. Where the river moved away, it left behind rich soil. The Mississippi Delta is the area of flat land that was regularly flooded by the river, and so this was some of the most fertile land in the world. In the mid-1800s, white settlers began to clear the forests and marshes of the region to make room for agriculture, but this work was exhausting, difficult, and often dangerous. Wealthy white landowners instead made enslaved Black people do most of the physical work. Then, when the land was cleared, they continued using the dehumanizing system of enslaved labor to plant the cotton that made white Mississippians some of the wealthiest people in the world. In 1850, half of all the millionaires in the United States lived in Natchez, Mississippi, alone, a city edged by both the Mississippi River and the Mississippi Delta, and the site of an active, brutal market where enslaved Black people were bought and sold.

When the Civil War ended in 1865, Black Americans could no longer be legally forced to work for free. White plantation owners of the Mississippi Delta needed to find new sources of cheap labor. Some Black people were incarcerated and forced to continue working without pay. Others began to work as sharecroppers in the same fields on which they were formerly enslaved. They were technically free, but sharecropping was not much different from enslavement. Sharecropping means renting some land from an owner in exchange for a "share" of the crops that you produce. Black sharecroppers were often required to buy their food and supplies on credit from the landowners or other merchants, with high rates of interest. Sharecroppers frequently found themselves deeply in debt. Most Black people did not want to work as sharecroppers, but many felt like they had few other options.

The cotton industry demanded ever more labor, and some white plantation owners began to look for additional people who would work in their fields. Some poor white people worked as sharecroppers, including people who had been in the South for a few generations. There were also new arrivals from the East Coast and people from even farther east—people from places like Italy. But there was another group of people whose numbers were rapidly growing in the West. And just like the railroad tycoons of the West considered using Black people as a replacement for Chinese labor, the plantation owners of the South saw Chinese people as a potential replacement for or addition to Black labor. Bringing Chinese people to the fields of the Deep South would solve two problems that existed in the eyes of many white Americans: it would reduce the number of Chinese people in the West and create a new source of labor in the South. Neither of these outcomes came to pass.

The first Chinese people arrived in the Mississippi Delta soon after the end of the Civil War. Most of them had first traveled to California from the same regions of southern China that the other Chinese Americans of the time had come from. Instead of establishing themselves in the West, these Chinese people were brought to Mississippi to work as share-croppers in the cotton fields.

We know that some Americans thought that Chinese people would be useful in the cotton fields by looking at documents from the time, including a political cartoon that was published in *Frank Leslie's Illustrated Newspaper* in 1869. This image is captioned "What shall we do with John Chinaman?" You will remember that "John Chinaman" was the name given to the stereotype of Chinese men at that time. On the left of the cartoon, an Irishman is shown holding a Chinese man by his long queue and thinking about throwing this man over a cliff toward a distant land labeled "China." The caption on the left reads, "What Pat would do with him." Pat was the name given to the stereotype of Irish men. In the picture, both Pat (the Irishman) and John Chinaman are drawn with stereotypically racist physical features. On the right of the cartoon, however, there is a different picture. A character that looks like a stereotypical Confederate colonel points off into the distance with a sinister look on his face. A signpost pointing in the same direction says, "Cheap labor wanted in the cotton fields SOUTH." The John Chinaman character, smiling, seems to be blindly heading off in the direction of the pointing. The caption on this side of the image reads, "What will be done with him." The cartoon suggests that the presence of Chinese people in the Western U.S. is a problem that must be solved. The cartoon also suggests that solidarity between marginalized people would never be possible, because it implies that Irish Americans would rather get rid of Chinese people altogether, even in violent ways. And the cartoon shows how some people believed that the

A political cartoon in Frank Leslie's Illustrated Newspaper *showing Irish and Chinese stereotypes.*

need for labor in the South's cotton fields offered a different path forward for Chinese Americans. The Chinese man, shown with slanted eyes, long pigtail, and dark skin, is portrayed as easy to manipulate—a pawn in the Confederate's game to find more labor for the plantation economy.

The Chinese men who were brought to work in cotton fields quickly realized that sharecropping was not an easy life or a good way to make a living. They started to find other sources of work, and many were successful. When Chinese Americans in the Mississippi Delta realized that they did not want to be sharecroppers, they had options that most Black Americans did not have. In California, laws had been passed to explicitly target Chinese mining income, communal living situations, and hairstyles. These laws criminalized Chinese people and limited their economic power. In the South, however, the laws that criminalized a racial group mostly focused on Black Americans. These laws, known as Black Codes, explicitly targeted African Americans, formerly enslaved people and their descendants. Because of the Black Codes, the Chinese Americans who had been employed as sharecroppers in Mississippi had more options than the Black Americans working the same fields.

The Chinese of the Deep South were also able to use their connections to Chinese people in other parts of the country to help their transition out of the fields. A network of Chinese Americans was starting to put down roots across the nation. Just as the powerful associations of California had created networks to support the Chinese community in the West, communities of Chinese Americans across the country continued to build networks that sustained their languages, religions, and cultural practices. These communities worked together to help Chinese Americans start businesses, navigate a complicated legal system, and otherwise share information and resources. Because these networks operated using Chinese languages, non-Chinese groups could not access these resources, and white people who might have been afraid of Chinese organizations were less able to monitor or disrupt these communities. These networks and organizations helped some Chinese people gain a sense of economic independence that was not available to other marginalized communities. By the end of the 1870s, many of the Chinese Americans in the Mississippi Delta had left the fields and opened grocery stores.

Even though they often weren't the explicit target of racial prejudice in the South, these Chinese

American grocery owners were not allowed to open their new stores in wealthy white neighborhoods. Instead, most found themselves serving the Black and poor white communities alongside whom they had just been working in the fields. Chinese grocery owners' futures now seemed brighter than they had when they were sharecroppers, but they did not find full acceptance or belonging. In many ways, Chinese people were starting to find themselves "in between" white and Black communities. Chinese people were not welcome in most white spaces, and the same racist prejudices that had existed about Chinese people out west remained wherever they were in the country. In historical documents about the Mississippi Delta from the time, both Chinese and Black people are typically described as "colored." While the language of "colored" might have lumped Chinese and Black communities under one label, each community faced different forms of discrimination. For the Chinese community, this discrimination increasingly had a single focus: white Americans' desire to exclude them.

LET'S THINK ABOUT THIS:

1. Divide and conquer is a strategy that keeps groups from organizing together to gain greater rights and power for all people. What other examples can you think of where people who had interests in common were put in conflict with each other, instead of working together?

2. How would you define "solidarity" in your own words? Why is it important? What are some examples of solidarity that you can think of from history and from today?

3. Can people have different backgrounds, experiences, and needs and still work in solidarity? What are some strategies people can use to work together in solidarity?

CHAPTER 4

A RACIAL HIERARCHY

Often when people talk about race and racism in the United States, it is by describing the relationship between white people and *people of color*. We don't talk as often about how racism also affects the relationships between racial and ethnic groups who aren't white. The idea of a *racial hierarchy* can help us understand how racism is a system that keeps communities of color in competition, even when white people aren't in the room. Let's look at a metaphor about something simple to first explain how hierarchies work, and then come back to talking about race.

One way people mentally organize things that are different is by creating something called a hierarchy, or a ranking. You might have a hierarchy of foods, with your favorites at the top, your least favorites at the bottom, and everything else somewhere in between. Now imagine that you are given the power to control all the meals served in your school's cafeteria. With this power, you would probably make sure that the things at the top of your food hierarchy are served the most often, and the things at the bottom of your food hierarchy are never served at all. Sounds pretty good, right? You'd get to eat your favorite things all the time, and you wouldn't have to eat any of the things you don't like.

Where do your food preferences—your food hierarchy—come from? Your preferences likely have a lot to do with where you grew up and the things your family eats. If your food hierarchy includes things from cultures different from your own, this is because you've had opportunities to try different types of food. In other words, the hierarchy that you have created for food is connected to your background and your previous experiences, and it is different from that of people who have different backgrounds and different experiences. If someone were to question your hierarchy, you might start to look for reasons to justify why your food hierarchy is the best. You might try to prove that your favorite foods are the most nutritious, whether that's true or not, or that all the foods at the bottom of your hierarchy are worthless and hated by everyone.

Now imagine that you have a classmate with a very different background from your own. They will likely have a different food hierarchy from yours. Because they've grown up eating different things in their home, something at the bottom of your food hierarchy might be at the top of theirs. It's easy to imagine that they'd be pretty disappointed by the decisions you've made about what is served and what isn't served in the cafeteria. And how would they feel if something at the top of their hierarchy is one of the foods that you have tried to claim is worthless and hated by everyone? They would probably feel like the school cafeteria is not a welcoming place.

And now imagine that you have several classmates who are allergic to many of the foods at the top of your hierarchy. The meals that you have decided should be served might actually turn out to be dangerous for some of your friends. Even without allergies, the new meal plan would probably turn out to be pretty bad for you, too. Most people's favorite foods don't represent a completely well-balanced diet, so the new menu might end up being harmful for everyone, including you, the person who had the power to make the decisions to begin with.

If you were to only use your own food preferences to decide what all of your classmates can and can't eat, it might make some people happy, but it would cause a lot of problems for others. The people who are happy will probably be ones who have similar food hierarchies to your own, which means they will probably have similar backgrounds to yours. These classmates will enjoy eating at school, even though the meals might not be the healthiest options for them either. They will feel like the cafeteria is a place where they belong, because the foods they see match their previous experiences and preferences.

But what about the students who are unfamiliar with the foods you've picked? What about the students who are allergic and could be hurt by these meals? Do you think that this new system would feel fair to them? Do you think the cafeteria would seem like a welcoming place?

As you can see, when one person or group of people creates a hierarchy based on their personal background, and then uses that hierarchy to make decisions that affect all people, it can lead to problems. Unfortunately, this has happened many times in history, about differences that are much more significant than food preferences. Before the 1800s in the United States, a firm hierarchy had been established about race.

A RACIAL HIERARCHY

From the earliest days of Europeans in America, many were fascinated with difference. It started with European people comparing themselves to Indigenous people, and seeing Indigenous people as inferior, or lower on the hierarchy. Next, these Europeans compared themselves to people from Africa in order to justify enslavement. Not all Europeans were always at the top of the racial hierarchy. In the early days of the United States, European Protestants, such as people from England or the Netherlands, saw themselves as higher on the hierarchy than European Catholics, like people from Ireland or Portugal. As the idea of "European" started changing into the idea of "white," different groups' positions in the hierarchy also started to change. The origins of "white" as a racial category are connected to the slave trade and justifying a racial hierarchy. You can learn more about this history in *Race to the Truth: Slavery and the African American Story* by Patricia Williams Dockery.

The fact that a group can be at a different level on a hierarchy at different times in history helps us to see that these hierarchies are made up to begin with. Just like your food hierarchy was determined by your personal preferences, the racial hierarchy of the United States was determined by the preferences of a small group of people who held power.

And just like you might have thought about ways you could prove that your food hierarchy was the best, some white people tried to use science to prove that white people were the best. Samuel Morton, a white doctor and scientist who was born in Philadelphia in 1799, was one of the famous men behind a philosophy known as *scientific racism*. Scientific racism tries to use the scientific method (something you might have learned about in school) to justify racial prejudice and racist systems. Samuel Morton is most famous for studying skulls to try to justify a racial hierarchy. He collected over a thousand human skulls and claimed that differences in some of the bone structures proved that some races were more intelligent than others. He even suggested that people of different races are from completely different species. Over the years, many scientists have looked at Samuel's skulls again and have pointed out that he

A portrait of Samuel Morton from around 1850.

made many errors in his measurements. They have also studied his arguments and pointed out the strong racial bias behind his conclusions. Before he began his skull studies, Samuel Morton already believed in a racial hierarchy that justified *white supremacy,* or the systems that work to keep white people at the top of the hierarchy. His biases led him to collect and write about his data in a way that supported his existing beliefs.

Scientific racism continues to this day. For example, some people look at differences in kids' test scores and argue that some races are biologically more intelligent than others. And these "scientific" justifications for racism continue to be proven false. For example, people who argue that some races are naturally smarter than others tend to ignore social and historical factors, like the histories of oppression you have read about in this book, that have limited some groups' access to high-quality education. They also ignore other factors that affect test scores like family income, access to nutritious food, school funding, parents' education background, and more. People who promote scientific racism are often trying to justify or prove the racial hierarchy, saying that racial hierarchies are not harmful but are natural and should continue forever.

You see, putting a group of people at the bottom of the racial hierarchy allows people with power to justify acts of cruelty against them. By saying that Indigenous Americans were lower on the racial hierarchy, white settlers could justify stealing Native lands for their own, even if it required violence and murder. The logic was: "We are more deserving of this land than they are." Earlier in this book you read how Native lands were taken by force during the Gold Rush, but it happened in many other places across the country. In the United States, Black Americans have almost always been put at the bottom of the racial hierarchy. By saying that Black people were inferior to white people, enslavers could justify owning humans, forcing them to work without pay, and buying and selling them to make a profit. We know that many white Americans held this view of Black inferiority because there are plenty of documents in which people explicitly said so. In 1785, Thomas Jefferson wrote that he suspected that Black people "are inferior to the whites in the endowments of both body and mind." Even Abraham Lincoln, a man known for his role in helping to end slavery, said in 1858, "There is a physical difference between the white and the black races which I believe will forever forbid the two races living together . . . while they do remain together there must be the position of superior and inferior, and I as much as any man am in favor having the superior position assigned to the white race."

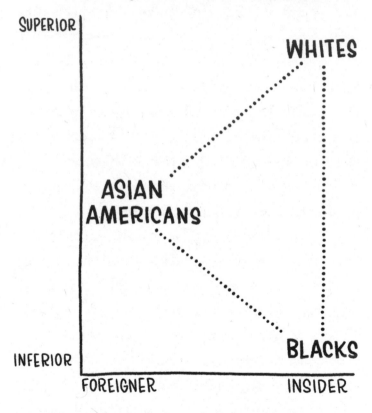

FIELD of RACIAL POSITIONS

Adapted from scholar Claire Jean Kim, this chart represents the racial hierarchy in another way. It shows that Asian Americans are higher on the hierarchy than Black Americans, but they are also seen as more foreign. Kim refers to this as the "racial triangulation of Asian Americans."

CHINESE AMERICANS have typically found themselves somewhere in the middle of the racial hierarchy. For example, while Chinese American laborers were often forced to work under unfair contracts, they were not enslaved. Their children could not be sold away from them. On the other hand, Chinese Americans faced different forms of discrimination from other groups. Because there were very few Chinese Americans in the United States for its first centuries, white Americans thought of them as complete outsiders.

Language and religion help us better understand the differences in how Black Americans and Chinese Americans were seen within the racial hierarchy during the mid-1800s. Black Americans, seen as most inferior and at the bottom of the hierarchy, were legally enslaved in many parts of the United States. The system of slavery is a cruel one, and it is designed to remove people's humanity. Enslaved people were forced to give up the languages and religious practices of their African ancestors. By the late 1800s, most Black Americans spoke only English and practiced Christianity. Many white Americans subjected Black Americans to extreme prejudice and racial terror, but by this time they rarely viewed them as "foreign."

These same people tended to see Chinese Americans as "more acceptable" than Black Americans, but they also saw them as so different and foreign that they would never belong.

HOMER PLESSY AND "SEPARATE BUT EQUAL"

The famous Supreme Court case known as *Plessy v. Ferguson* can help us to better understand both the racial hierarchy and the view of Chinese people as *perpetual foreigners*. (You can read more about the perpetual foreigner stereotype by returning to Chapter 1 of this book.) You might have learned about *Plessy v. Ferguson* in school, because it created the legal precedent for a segregated system known as "separate but equal." A precedent is something that sets the example or the rule for what should happen in the future. The Supreme Court's decision in *Plessy v. Ferguson* set the precedent for legal *segregation,* the rule that people could legally be required to stay apart simply because of their race.

In 1890, Louisiana passed a state law called the Separate Car Act, requiring that white and Black passengers sit in segregated train cars. Two years later, in New Orleans, Louisiana, a man named Homer Plessy bought a first-class ticket to sit in the section of a train reserved for white people. You see, a multiracial group of Louisiana residents was upset with this new segregation law, and they had organized a committee to use civil disobedience to do something about it. If they could get the right person in trouble under this law, they thought they could convince the Supreme Court that the law was unfair and should be overturned. The committee believed that Homer Plessy would be the right person for this job.

Historians aren't sure exactly what year it was, but in either 1862 or 1863, Homer Plessy was born to a French-speaking family in Louisiana. Homer had seven great-grandparents who were white and one who was Black, and he was born free. Even so, because of his one Black great-grandparent, he would have been considered "colored." But when Homer was growing up, this didn't seem to matter as much as it had even a few years before.

Homer Plessy grew up in Louisiana in the period right after the Civil War known as *Radical Reconstruction*. You might not know that there was a time in the 1800s when things were closer to equal than most people today realize they were, and that's the time Homer grew up in. During Radical Reconstruction it seemed like the old racial hierarchy, with white people on the top and Black people on the bottom, was starting to change for the better. In Louisiana when Homer Plessy was young, Black children could go to school with white children. Black men could vote and run for political office. People of different races could legally marry. We often think that people have only ever gained rights as time has gone on, but there have been times in the past when traditionally marginalized groups had more rights than we realize, only to have these rights taken away again.

Before the Civil War, the American South had been controlled by white, landowning men who supported enslavement and opposed the Union government. When the war ended in 1865 and the Confederacy fell, these men were stripped of their power. This began Radical Reconstruction, the time that Homer Plessy grew up in. But Radical Reconstruction did not last for long. In 1877, barely a decade after the Civil War ended, many former Confederates regained power. They had been able to use their wealth and influence at the national level to argue that they, the wealthy, white men of the South, should once again be firmly positioned at the top of the racial hierarchy. These men quickly started undoing laws that had allowed people like Homer Plessy to live with relative freedom, and they started writing new laws to create further discrimination. They had experienced what it might be like to no longer be at the top, and they wanted to make sure it would never happen again. Even though enslavement was now legally over, they wanted to create new laws to keep people of color "in their place." The system commonly known as *Jim Crow* had begun.

Homer Plessy, having watched so many freedoms get taken away from himself and others like him, decided to resist. When Homer got on the train in 1892 and sat down in the section for white people, he knew that he would probably be arrested, but he was prepared for that. In fact, that was his plan all along. He and the people who had planned this resistance wanted to use Homer's act of civil disobedience to prove that the segregation law was racist and unfair. Train conductors asked Homer Plessy to move to a car reserved for Black people, and when he refused, they had him arrested. His case eventually made its way to the Supreme Court of the United States. Homer Plessy and people who held his views hoped that the court would see that what had happened to Homer was wrong. They hoped that the court would rule that segregation was unconstitutional, and that they would ban laws like this from being created in the future.

The story of *Plessy v. Ferguson* does not have a happy ending. In 1896, eight Supreme Court justices participated in the ruling, all of whom were white men. Seven of these justices ruled against Homer Plessy, saying that there was no problem with legal segregation by race. The decision of these seven men allowed for the next several decades of legal segregation on buses, at water fountains, in schools, and in many other places. Only one justice, a man named John Harlan, said that Homer should be allowed to sit anywhere on the train because racial segregation was wrong. In his dissenting, or disagreeing, opinion, John wrote that the United States government should guarantee "equality before the law of all citizens of the United States, without regard to race."

Today, many people will reference this part of John Harlan's dissent as a strong statement against racism. John Harlan is sometimes known as "the Great Dissenter." His words are used as evidence that, even at the time, there were white people who knew that a racial hierarchy is wrong. People today are far less likely to share something else that John Harlan included in what he wrote about *Plessy v. Ferguson*. By reading his full dissent, we can see how Black people's rights and Chinese people's rights have often been treated in relation to one another, and how

Chinese people have been seen as perpetual foreigners. Immediately after writing that the government should treat all citizens equally, John Harlan began the next paragraph of his dissent with, "There is a race so different from our own that we do not permit those belonging to it to become citizens of the United States. Persons belonging to it are, with few exceptions, absolutely excluded from our country. I allude to the Chinese race."

MARTHA LUM, LEGALLY "COLORED"

The Supreme Court's decision in *Plessy v. Ferguson* said that segregation was legal. Although John Harlan's dissent said that Chinese people are excluded from the United States, the court's decision in *Plessy v. Ferguson* mainly focused on segregation between Black and white Americans. It would take another Supreme Court case to explicitly rule on where Chinese and other Asian Americans should fall in the racial hierarchy. This case was *Lum v. Rice*, and it brings our focus back to the Deep South. The case focused on a Chinese American girl named Martha Lum who tried to go to a white school in a small town called Rosedale, Mississippi.

In 1904, a man named Lum Jeu Gong settled in the Mississippi Delta. There, he married a Chinese American woman named Katherine Wong. Katherine's family was already established in Mississippi. Like many of the Chinese Americans of the region that you've read about, her father owned and operated a grocery store that mostly served the Black community. After they were married, Lum Jeu Gong also opened a grocery store. The couple had two daughters. The younger, Martha, was born in 1915. The Lum family made a good living in the grocery business, and in 1923 they were able to buy a home in the little Delta town of Rosedale.

Rosedale, Mississippi, is on the western edge of the Mississippi Delta and sits right up along the mighty river. Like most other Delta towns, its fortunes were tied up in cotton. The first European settlers of the region started cotton plantations that relied on Black people's labor, first from enslaved people and later from sharecroppers. Eventually, the town also became a railroad hub, storing cotton from the wider Delta region and sending it on trains to be sold in the North. If you are a fan of a music style called the blues, you might have heard the name of Rosedale before. The town shows up in many blues songs, and there's even a legend that says the famous blues musician Robert Johnson sold his soul to the devil at the crossroads just outside of Rosedale in exchange for learning to master the guitar. Several towns in the Mississippi Delta claim that *they* are the real location of the crossroads, but Rosedale is one of the more popular theories about where (and if) this transaction really happened.

When the Lum family moved to Rosedale, the town's population was somewhere just under two thousand people. Between around 1910 and 1970, six million Black people left the South to escape prejudiced Jim Crow laws and the ongoing threat of racial terror, a massive movement of people known as the *Great Migration*. But in the 1920s, when the Lums moved there, Mississippi was still majority African American. Even though more than half of Mississippians were Black, almost all the power and wealth in the state was controlled by white people. Chinese people like the Lums had a lot more access to the white community than Black people did. Martha Lum's mother, Katherine, was an active participant in a white church. Many white people in Rosedale felt that because Mrs. Lum was a devoted Christian, she was an acceptable member of the community, in spite of being Chinese American. Some people might have even felt proud that Christianity had "saved" this

Chinese woman. At the time, newspaper articles regularly described Chinese people as soulless heathens, and the white community of Rosedale would have been familiar with this stereotype. At first, it seemed that the family was also welcomed in the white education system. There were two schools in the town, one for white students and one for "colored" students, which served the community's Black population. When the Lums first moved to Rosedale, Martha and her older sister, Berda, enrolled at the white school, where they spent the 1923–1924 school year.

Even though the Lum family experienced far less prejudice than the local Black community faced, they were not fully accepted into white society. The Lums' grocery store served the Black community so that it would not compete with white-owned businesses that served the white community. Chinese grocery stores served a purpose for both the Black and white communities of the Delta, operating almost as a middle area within the racial hierarchy. Records show that some Chinese grocery owners referred to their Black customers with terms like "Mr." and "Mrs.," a level of respect they would rarely receive from a white shopkeeper. Chinese grocery stores did not ask Black customers to pay in company credit, a system that many plantation owners used with sharecroppers who worked on their land. And, because Chinese grocery stores were opened in Black communities, they were more convenient and easier to access than stores in the wealthier, whiter parts of town. At the same time, however, many Chinese store owners held anti-Black beliefs and saw themselves as above their Black neighbors and customers. They sometimes treated their customers with suspicion or outright hostility. Many believed that they could advance their own position by disadvantaging their Black neighbors and customers. In these cases, they actively resisted forming bonds or better connections with Black communities in order to gain more acceptance from the white community.

Chinese grocery stores served a greater purpose for the wealthier white communities of the Mississippi Delta. Chinese stores operated in Black communities, which many white store owners believed was not a practical way to earn a lot of money. More to the point, however, if white people never had to serve Black people in their stores, then there would never be a need to fully integrate the Black and white communities. Chinese people could serve as a wedge, maintaining segregation between Black people and white people forever.

In other words, the presence of this small community of Chinese grocery store owners helped to maintain the racial hierarchy. Black people were rarely allowed to enter white society. Most were expected to work the worst jobs, to live in segregated, run-down housing, and to attend badly funded, falling-apart schools, if they were fortunate enough to attend school at all. While Black people would spend their money within the Black community and at white- and Chinese-owned businesses, money rarely moved in the other direction. White and Chinese people rarely spent money at Black-owned businesses. This situation kept Chinese people above Black people in the racial hierarchy, and some Chinese families became quite wealthy through their trade in poor Black communities. The Lum family was one of the families that became financially comfortable through this arrangement.

But Chinese people were still not as high as white people in the racial hierarchy. After all, wealthy white people at the top of the racial hierarchy were the ones creating this whole system in the first place. They had created racist policies that affected where Black and Chinese people were allowed to live and work, whom they could marry, and whether or not they could hold elected office. (The answer? They couldn't.) Some white people were uncomfortable with the somewhat "acceptable" status that Chinese Americans like the

Lums had found in white spaces like churches and schools. These people felt that Chinese people needed to fall back down the racial hierarchy. They needed to be "put in their place."

At the beginning of the 1924 school year, Martha Lum once again enrolled in the white school in Rosedale. Partway through her first day of school, however, she was told that she would have to leave. A group of people known as the board of trustees were in charge of making decisions about the school, and they had decided that Martha needed to go to the "colored" school. Chinese people were not white, after all, and the board did not care that Martha had already attended a white school for a whole year without a problem. Martha, unlike her sister, Berda, loved school, and she had been a hardworking, well-behaved student. She and her family were devastated that she would not be allowed to return. They decided to fight back and try to get Martha re-enrolled at Rosedale's white school.

At the end of the day, the story of *Lum v. Rice* is a story about the racial hierarchy and anti-Black racism. The Lum family was not upset about Martha being turned away from the white school because they believed that segregation was wrong in and of itself. They were more upset that the board of trustees was saying that a girl like Martha Lum did not deserve to belong to white society, and that her status was equal to the Black students who attended the "colored" school. If the family agreed with the board's decision and enrolled her in the "colored" school, they would basically be saying they agreed that Martha did not deserve the privileges of white society. The Lum family was keenly aware of what it was like to live at the bottom of the racial hierarchy—they saw Black families struggling all around them—and they did not want their children to have to do the same.

The Lum family hired a white lawyer to try to overturn the school board's decision. The man they hired was named Earl L. Brewer, and he had been governor of the state of Mississippi less than ten years before. Earl Brewer argued that the "colored" school had been created to serve the "colored" race—in other words, it had been created to serve Black students. He argued that Martha, being Chinese, was not "colored." Since there was no school in Rosedale that had been created to serve Chinese students, he argued that Martha would have to be allowed at Rosedale Consolidated High School, the one that served white students. A district court judge agreed with Earl Brewer and said that Martha should be allowed to re-enroll at her former school.

The board of trustees was unhappy with the district court's decision. They believed that the Rosedale schools should only serve white students, and Martha, being Chinese, should not be welcome. One of the board members, a man named Greek Rice, led the way to *appeal* the district court's decision, or to try to get a higher court to review and change the original ruling. (Court cases get their names from the main people arguing on either side. In the case of *Lum v. Rice,* the Lum family was on one side and Greek Rice, leading the school board of trustees in Rosedale, was on the other.) The board appealed the district court's decision to the Supreme Court of Mississippi. This time, things didn't go the Lum family's way. Earl Brewer had made a few critical mistakes. His logic was inconsistent and changed throughout his argument. Part of his case rested on the idea that Martha was not "colored," and he repeated many racist stereotypes of Black people to try to prove his points. He did not talk enough about how Martha, a United States citizen, should be granted the same "equal protection" under the Constitution as other citizens. Equal protection was a key part of the argument used a few decades later in the case *Brown v. Board of Education,* which finally overturned legal segregation on the basis of race. Had Earl Brewer made that argument instead of the ones he went with, Martha Lum's name might have become famous for ending the unjust system of "separate but equal." Instead, very few people know her name today.

The Mississippi Supreme Court ruled on the side of Greek Rice and the board, saying they were right for keeping Martha out of the white school. The court agreed with arguments that Chinese people, by not being white, are in fact "colored," and so Martha should rightfully have to attend the "colored" school. The Lum family appealed again, and the case found itself in front of the Supreme Court of the United States, the highest court in the land. This time, a new lawyer would be arguing the family's case, but it did not matter. The U.S. Supreme Court agreed with the Mississippi Supreme Court. In a 9–0 decision, they ruled that Chinese people were officially "colored" and that the board of trustees was justified in stopping her from going to a white school.

The Supreme Court's ruling said that school segregation on the basis of race was perfectly legal, a ruling with the potential to affect millions of students across the United States. But the ruling only indirectly affected Martha herself. It takes many years for a case to work its way through various courts. By the time the Supreme Court ruling was finally issued, the Lum family had moved across the Mississippi River to Arkansas. Arkansas was less strict in its rules about school segregation, and the family had found a white school that would take Martha. Elsewhere in the Mississippi Delta, Chinese communities opened their own schools, creating yet another separation in a school system that was already divided by race. The court's decision in *Lum v. Rice* was used for decades to come whenever someone tried to make a legal argument against school segregation. The Supreme Court had ruled that there was no problem with what the Rosedale schools did when they turned Martha away, and this decision was used to justify segregation on the basis of race until the policy was finally overturned in 1954 by their decision in *Brown v. Board of Education*.

THE STORY OF *LUM V. RICE* is a story of divide and conquer. Chinese communities and Black communities in Rosedale had more in common than most people realized. Although their situations and the specific injustices that they faced were different, both communities were being kept from true belonging and power by the same forces. These forces—centered in the wealthy, landowning white community—did whatever it took to keep Chinese and Black communities from joining together in solidarity. These groups outnumbered the white community, and if they had joined together, then white people's security at the top of the hierarchy would have been in danger. Many new Chinese immigrants felt that the only way to be accepted in their new country was to gain the acceptance of white people, and that the best way to gain this acceptance would be to distance themselves from Black Americans. But why did it have to be this way? Why did one group of people, a white minority in the case of Mississippi in the 1920s, have the power to decide where everyone else should fall on the racial hierarchy?

In the Mississippi Delta, Black and Chinese Americans were expected to live in the same, less comfortable neighborhoods than white Americans. Black and Chinese Americans were required to attend the same, less funded schools than white Americans. But rather than trying to work together to overturn a system that kept both groups in a position of oppression, many Chinese Americans, including the Lum family, spent much of their energy trying to make the case that they were better than Black people. Not only did they have few examples of cross-racial solidarity, solidarity was risky. Those who did try to build connections across racial lines were often shunned, or worse. So, instead of finding solidarity, many Chinese Americans tried to find belonging by agreeing that the racial hierarchy was okay, as long as they weren't at the very bottom. But of course, as the Lum family found out, being above one group in the racial hierarchy is not the same as being at the top. In the end, the racial hierarchy hurts all of us.

LET'S THINK ABOUT THIS:

1. How would you describe the racial hierarchy in your own words? Where have you seen or heard people support racial hierarchies? Where have you seen or heard people resist racial hierarchies?

2. Some people say that people have only ever gained rights over time, but after the end of Radical Reconstruction, Black Americans lost many of the rights that they had previously held. What other examples can you think of when people lost rights instead of gaining them? Why do you think this happens?

3. What examples of divide and conquer do you see in this chapter? What examples of solidarity do you see?

CHAPTER 5

EXCLUSION

You might have noticed that the early sections of this book mostly focus on Chinese men, not Chinese people in general. This is because almost all of the miners, the railroad workers, the laundry workers, the plantation laborers, the Chinatown shopkeepers, and the other early Chinese Americans were men. You see, the immigration stories of early Chinese Americans often have a lot to do with gender. The risky task of traveling over the ocean to find one's fortune was seen as more appropriate for men than women. The hard work that was available to Chinese people was also seen as men's work. Businesses that were willing to hire Chinese workers, such as railroads, coal mines, and plantations, felt that men would be better at doing manual labor. And, for Chinese people who were able to be their own bosses, like by running a laundry, even owning a business was more accessible to men than women. It was difficult or impossible for women to open a bank account or sign the lease to rent a building, so most Chinese women were financially dependent on men.

But there was another reason that most of the early Chinese immigrants were men. The white people who felt that Chinese people were dangerous, dirty, and less than human did not want Chinese people to put down roots in the United States. They were happy with the idea that Chinese people might feel more connected to China than to their new country. It wasn't just that some people thought that Chinese people were perpetual foreigners—they actively passed laws to keep it that way.

THE PAGE ACT

In 1873, a white man named Horace Page was elected to the U.S. House of Representatives, representing California's second congressional district. Like many powerful white men in California at the time, Horace was originally from the East Coast. Today, Horace

Page is most famous for his racist viewpoints and his role in two laws that would shape the Chinese American experience for many years to come. Horace was outspoken in his anti-Black racism, and he was also steeped in the anti-Chinese racism that swirled around California at the time. Men like Horace Page wanted Chinese people around for their cheap labor, but they also wanted to stop Chinese people from staying too long or starting to see themselves as Americans.

In 1875, Horace Page introduced something called the Page Act. Yes, it's named for him. Page said his new law was about protecting jobs for white Americans by limiting the number of foreigners who could be brought to the United States for their labor. But in reality, the Page Act was used to ban the entry of almost all Chinese women to the United States. Before 1875, most people could travel freely in and out of the country. The Page Act changed all of that. The Page Act was part of the *backlash,* or the strong negative reaction, to people's free movement across American borders. Like with the backlash to Radical Reconstruction, some people believed that those who were lower on the racial hierarchy now had too much freedom. People like Horace Page worked to pass laws that would take these freedoms away. In fact, the Page Act was the first federal legislation that restricted, or set limits on, the entry of a group of people to the United States, and Chinese women were its targets.

The logic of the Page Act was simple: It would limit the number of Chinese women in the United States, and thus stop Chinese people from becoming included in American society by keeping them from starting families. Chinese men would come to work in the United States while they were young and healthy enough to do the hard labor the new country needed. Then, when they were ready to start families of their own, they would have to go back to China to find a wife. The law would make it very difficult for Chinese men to start relationships in America with women who shared their same language, religion, and cultural traditions. Marrying or starting relationships across racial lines was, at best, frowned upon. In many states it was explicitly illegal. The Page Act would make it even less likely that Chinese people would have children born in the United States who might grow up seeing themselves as Americans.

And there was another reason lawmakers like Horace Page wanted to limit the number of Chinese women in the United States. One of the common stereotypes about Chinese women at the time was that they were prostitutes who would seduce, corrupt, and spread diseases to white American men. Even President Ulysses S. Grant, the celebrated hero of the American Civil War, knew these stereotypes about Chinese women. In his 1875 State of the Union address, President Grant described what he saw as a great evil: "the importation of Chinese women, but few of whom are brought to our shores to pursue honorable or useful occupations." In other words, President Grant was saying that most Chinese women were being brought for dishonorable, useless purposes— code for sex work. The Page Act was successful in limiting the number of Chinese women who came to the United States. After the law was passed, fewer than 5 percent of the Chinese people in the U.S. were women.

In spite of the law's effectiveness, people like Horace Page were not satisfied with the restrictions of the Page Act. Not even ten years after the Page Act had been signed into law, legislators were working on new policies that would go even further in keeping Chinese people from entering or putting down roots in the United States. In 1882, none other than Horace Page himself introduced a new law: the Chinese Exclusion Act. Lawmakers in favor of the Chinese Exclusion Act took to the floors of Congress to share their beliefs that Chinese people were "strange," "peculiar," "half-civilized," "dangerous," and "capable of causing ruin." This time, the law was not vague about who it was targeting. The goal of the law is right in its name. The purpose of the Chinese Exclusion Act was to exclude Chinese people from the United States.

THE CHINESE EXCLUSION ACT

On May 6, 1882, President Chester A. Arthur signed the Chinese Exclusion Act into law. Many white Americans cheered this new law. It was common to hear people repeating slogans like "No more Chinese!" Even newspapers ran headlines like "Hip! Hurrah! Chinese Excluded." While some Americans of all racial backgrounds did not agree with the Chinese Exclusion Act, it seemed like most people were more than happy to keep Chinese people out of America forever.

A portrait of President Chester A. Arthur in 1881.

Of course, President Arthur's signature of the law must not have felt good at all to the Chinese people who wanted to come to the country or to the Chinese Americans who already thought of the United States as home.

The Chinese Exclusion Act banned all new Chinese immigration. There were a few exceptions that let Chinese merchants and professionals continue to arrive in the country, but this was a very small group of people, and it was clear that they were not welcome to remain forever. Almost all of the Chinese immigrants at the time were working-class people seeking employment as laborers, and this group was now excluded. The Chinese Exclusion Act also banned people of Chinese ancestry from becoming United States citizens. At first the Chinese Exclusion Act was written to last for only ten years, but it would remain the law of the land for the next six decades.

TEN YEARS AFTER President Arthur first signed it into law, the Chinese Exclusion Act was about to expire. Chinese people would no longer be stopped from coming to the United States. Anti-Chinese lawmakers wanted to make sure that Chinese people would continue to be excluded. By then, Horace Page was no longer a U.S. Representative, but there were other people who held his same beliefs. In 1892, a man named Thomas Geary, another U.S. Representative from California, introduced something called the Geary Act. Like the Page Act was named after Horace Page, the Geary Act gets its name from Thomas Geary. The Geary Act renewed the Chinese Exclusion Act, and it was easily passed through both houses of Congress. In May of that same year, President Benjamin Harrison signed it into law.

The Geary Act didn't just extend the Chinese Exclusion Act, it made the law even worse for Chinese people. Under this new version of the Chinese Exclusion Act, it did not matter whether a person was born in China, the United States, or somewhere else— anyone with Chinese ancestry had to submit to restrictions that did not apply to people of other backgrounds. At all times, anyone with Chinese heritage had to carry a paper proving that they were legally allowed to be in the country. If a Chinese person was caught without their paper, they could be removed from the United States or forced to work in a labor camp. The Geary Act also made it illegal for Chinese people to be witnesses in legal trials. This meant that Chinese people had fewer ways to stand up for themselves and each other in court. Because of these new laws, some Chinese people were unfairly convicted of crimes they did not commit, and others were unable to seek justice when crimes were committed against them.

OF COURSE, there were many Chinese Americans and other people of various backgrounds who saw the Page Act, the Chinese Exclusion Act, and the Geary Act as discriminatory and unjust. In 1869, Frederick Douglass, a formerly enslaved Black person and a fierce advocate for racial justice, gave a speech in Boston. This speech is often referred to as "The Composite Nation." In this speech, he described the divide and conquer tactics of wealthy white Americans:

Frederick Douglass pictured in 1864.

"They would rather have laborers who will work for nothing; but as they cannot get [Black Americans] on these terms, they want Chinamen who, they hope, will work for next to nothing." Frederick Douglass urged Americans of all backgrounds to reject the racial hierarchy. He spoke about the long-standing, unjust treatment of Indigenous and Black Americans and warned his listeners about the efforts being taken to treat Chinese Americans unjustly. He described how this injustice was already happening in California and was likely to spread across the country: "Already has California assumed a bitterly unfriendly attitude toward the Chinamen. Already has she driven them from her altars of justice. Already has she stamped them as outcasts and handed them over to popular contempt and vulgar jest. Already are they the constant victims of cruel harshness and brutal violence."

In his speech Frederick Douglass repeated many of the existing stereotypes about Chinese people and other groups, but he also said that these stereotypes should not matter and that the United States should be a place where all people can belong. After all, he said, "There are such things in the world as human rights." By explicitly showing his support for Chinese people, Frederick Douglass was naming and resisting divide and conquer strategies. He knew the dangers of divide and conquer, and how these strategies are used to keep people lower on the racial hierarchy from working together to change the system so that it is fairer for everyone. Frederick Douglass's example shows that there have always been people from different racial backgrounds who have stood up for each other's rights.

● ● ●

OTHER PEOPLE TRIED to resist the discrimination against Chinese people through the court system. In 1893, the United States Supreme Court heard a case known as *Fong Yue Ting v. United States*. The Geary Act had introduced *deportation* to the United States, or forcibly removing someone from a country who is not there legally. *Fong Yue Ting v. United States* challenged the Geary Act, arguing that deportation was an unfair form of punishment. The people in this case had been arrested for not having the correct papers that said they were allowed to be in the country. Getting a paper was not that easy. Among other things, the Geary Act required that a white witness confirm a Chinese person's identity before the paper could be issued. The Fong Yue Ting case argued that this was an unfair requirement and an unjust reason to arrest people. Instead of overturning the racist law, the Supreme Court decided to let it stand. *Fong Yue Ting v. United States* became a *precedent,* or a guide for how decisions should be made in the future. Other cases that tried to challenge the Geary Act were also unsuccessful. The court's support of these laws made them harder to undo, and future court rulings pointed to these precedents to justify systems like immigrant detention and deportation.

Today's immigration system in the United States

is deeply connected to the ways the country thought about Chinese immigration in the 1800s. Systems like immigrant detention and deportation continue to this day. These systems have been enforced in different ways across different groups at various points in U.S. history, depending on who is seen as welcome or unwelcome at any given time. Newspapers in the late 1800s tried to build popular support for Chinese exclusion by publishing headlines that described Chinese immigration as an "invasion." Today, words like "invasion" are sometimes used to describe migration of people coming to the United States from places like Central and South America. Just like in the 1800s, this word suggests that these people do not belong and should be feared, and the legal systems that were used to detain and deport Chinese Americans more than a hundred years ago continue to be used to control and reject immigrants from other groups today.

THE CHINESE INVASION!
They Are Coming, 900,000 Strong.

TO BE PUBLISHED IN A FEW DAYS,
with Maps, Illustrations and Stereoscopic
Views. What are you going to do about it?
Nations of the earth take warning.   a27-1t*

A headline in the San Francisco Chronicle from August 27, 1873.

WONG KIM ARK, AN AMERICAN BY BIRTH

Not every legal challenge to Chinese exclusion failed. While some cases created systems that have been used to keep people from having equal rights, other cases helped expand rights to more people. One of the most important of these cases is *United States v. Wong Kim Ark.*

In 1873, Wong Kim Ark was born in San Francisco, California. His parents had arrived in the U.S. at a time when migration was more open, before the Page Act restricted the immigration of Chinese women and the Chinese Exclusion Act restricted the immigration of all Chinese people. By the time Wong Kim Ark was born, his father was a merchant who ran a store on Sacramento Street in San Francisco's Chinatown. Kim Ark was born in the apartment his family shared, right upstairs from their shop.

Wong Kim Ark's parents, who had been born in China, had no opportunity to become U.S. citizens. Since 1790, naturalized citizenship—or citizenship that someone gains after moving to a new country— was only open to free white people. Eighty years later, the Naturalization Act of 1870 had opened naturalization to people of African descent as well, but Chinese and other Asian people, as well as some people from other backgrounds, were still prevented from becoming citizens.

Within the first ten years of Wong Kim Ark's life, both the Page Act and the Chinese Exclusion Act were signed into law. Over the following years, life became increasingly challenging for many Chinese American families who had made their homes in America's Chinatowns. They faced intense social prejudice. The same year that Kim Ark was born, the chant "The Chinese must go!" had become a common rallying cry from white Americans who were afraid that Chinese people would take too many of the country's jobs. They didn't care that many jobs

A photograph of Wong Kim Ark from an immigration document in 1904.

that Chinese people held were ones that white people had not wanted to apply for, like working on the railroads. They had been told that Chinese people were to blame for economic problems, and so they wanted Chinese exclusion. Men like Horace Page and Thomas Geary, who held these same prejudiced beliefs and held positions of power, then passed laws that further reminded people like the Wong family that they were not welcome.

In 1890, when Wong Kim Ark was a teenager, his parents decided that life in their new country had become too difficult to manage. They had come to the United States to try to make a better life for themselves and for their families, but their new country did not want them. Wong Kim Ark's family, and thousands of other Chinese Americans like them, once again boarded ships to cross the Pacific Ocean. This time, they were heading in the other direction. Kim Ark and his family returned to China, to the region of Guangdong Province known as Taishan (sometimes spelled Toisan or Toishan).

In a village near his family's ancestral home, Wong Kim Ark met a woman named Yee Shee. They were soon married and conceived their first child, a son. Pretty quickly, however, Kim Ark decided that he needed to return to the United States. He had worked as a cook in Chinatown, and he could earn a better living in San Francisco than in his family's village. After all, Wong Kim Ark had been born in the United States and had lived there his whole life. While his parents would have had connections and opportunities in China, Kim Ark must have felt a bit like a stranger in what was supposed to be his home-land. The United States was the only homeland he'd ever known.

Wong Kim Ark's decision to leave China was prob-ably not an easy one. Returning to the United States meant leaving his pregnant wife in Taishan. Because of the Chinese Exclusion Act, she was not allowed to enter the United States. Kim Ark would have to make the journey alone, sending the money he could earn in Chinatown back to China to support his new family. Less than a year after his last ocean voyage, and before his first son was born, he boarded a ship to return to San Francisco once again. When he arrived in California, Kim Ark let the border agents know that he had been born in the United States. He was allowed through without much issue.

A few years later, in 1894, Wong Kim Ark had earned enough money to afford a visit to his family in Taishan. In the four years since he'd been back in the United States, anti-Chinese prejudice had only continued to grow. The Geary Act had been passed, and Kim Ark knew that he would need to carry a paper that proved his identity and that he belonged in America. Before he left for Taishan, Wong Kim Ark prepared a document that included his photograph and information about where he had been born. Kim Ark even got the necessary signatures from three white people swearing that he had been born in San Francisco and that they knew him well. This paper was signed and sealed by a public official called a *notary public* on November 5, 1894, meaning that it was certified as a real, official, and legal document by the state of California. With paper in hand, Wong Kim

Ark set off on the voyage to see his family in China, confident that he would once again be allowed re-entry to the United States after his visit. After all, he had been allowed through the last time and now, with this official document, he surely would have no issue.

In Taishan, Wong Kim Ark was reunited with his family. He met his eldest son for the first time. Kim Ark and his wife conceived their second son. Soon, however, he would have to return to the United States to continue to work. In August of 1895, Kim Ark once again arrived at the Port of San Francisco. This time, things didn't go so easily for Wong Kim Ark.

In 1893, a white man named John H. Wise had become the Collector of Customs in San Francisco. In this job, John had the power to decide what—and who—came through the border of the United States at one of its largest ports. John Wise had been born in Virginia to a famously pro-slavery family. Since becoming Collector of Customs, John had made it much harder for Chinese people to enter the United States, including people like Wong Kim Ark who had been born in the U.S. to begin with. When Kim Ark arrived on the ship the SS *Coptic* that August of 1895, John Wise did not care that he had been born in the United States and that he was carrying a paper that backed up his claim. John Wise did not care that three white people had signed Wong Kim Ark's document, and he did not care that the paper had been certified by a notary public. John Wise said that Wong Kim Ark's parents were Chinese, and so Kim Ark was Chinese, and so, under the Chinese Exclusion Act, he should not be allowed to enter the country of his birth.

Because of his job, John Wise had a lot of individual power to restrict the entry of Chinese people to the United States. There were many Americans who wanted to make sure that future people who held John's position would make the same choices. They were looking for a case like Wong Kim Ark's to try to get the courts to turn these individual decisions into actual law. In the decade since the Chinese Exclusion Act was passed, people like Wong Kim Ark, who were born in the United States to Chinese parents, existed in a sort of gray area. Like with Kim Ark's first return to California, these people had sometimes been allowed through the U.S. border without issue. People who disagreed with John Wise thought it was correct to allow these Chinese Americans to continue to come to the United States. These people believed that the most powerful American document—the Constitution of the United States of America—was on their side, giving people like Wong Kim Ark the right to freely enter and remain in the country.

The Fourteenth Amendment to the Constitution, ratified after the end of the Civil War, said that: "All persons born or naturalized in the United States . . . are citizens of the United States and of the State wherein they reside." In other words, anyone born in the United States was a citizen of the United States. The Fourteenth Amendment had been written to guarantee citizenship to formerly enslaved Black Americans, and many people thought it applied to people like Wong Kim Ark as well. Hadn't he, too, been born in the United States? But other people thought that the Chinese Exclusion Act outweighed the Fourteenth Amendment. They felt that people like Kim Ark could never be citizens because of their parents' Chinese citizenship. Men like John Wise seemed to take pleasure in excluding Chinese Americans. He even wrote racist letters and poems bragging about the people he deported to China. If John Wise and people who held his point of view could get the Supreme Court to rule that citizenship is passed down from parents, and not based on where someone is born, then the gray area would not be gray anymore. Chinese people like Wong Kim

Ark would be permanently prevented from entering the United States, regardless of where they were born.

AFTER JOHN WISE STOPPED Wong Kim Ark's entry to the United States, Kim Ark was forced to stay on a steamship out in San Francisco Bay for five months while his case was being decided. The power of the United States government was against him. It might seem like Kim Ark didn't have a chance, and that he would never again be allowed entry to his home country. But he also had a powerful force on his side: the associations. The Six Companies, the same group of associations that supported Ho Ah Kow in the case that ended the practice of cutting off queues, once again gathered their resources. They threw all of their power behind supporting Wong Kim Ark's case, including providing the legal representation to argue on his behalf.

A California-born man of Irish ancestry named Thomas D. Riordan was a longtime attorney for the Chinese Associations of San Francisco, arguing many cases in favor of rights for Chinese people and organizations. Kim Ark's case was first heard in front of a district court, and Thomas Riordan argued strongly that Wong Kim Ark was a U.S. citizen and should be treated as such. Thomas referenced several earlier trials that had ruled in favor of Chinese immigration, as well as the citizenship clause of the Fourteenth Amendment. On January 3, 1896, the district court could see no alternative. They ruled that Wong Kim Ark, having been born in the United States, was a United States citizen.

The lawyers for the United States government were not happy with the district court's decision, and so they appealed to the Supreme Court. Again, they wanted a court to rule that Wong Kim Ark and people like him were not, and never would be, U.S. citizens. If they got their way, not only would Kim Ark never again be allowed to enter the United States, but all Chinese people could be forced to leave the United States and be sent to China, even if the U.S. was the only country they had ever known.

This time, Thomas Riordan was joined by two other white attorneys, Maxwell Evarts and J. Hubley Ashton. These men argued forcefully in favor of Wong Kim Ark's right to enter his country. Kim Ark's attorneys made it clear that the Fourteenth Amendment plainly stated that people born in the United States were citizens, and the Supreme Court agreed. On March 28, 1898, almost three years after Kim Ark had tried to return to the United States for the second time, the Supreme Court ruled 6–2 that the

Chinese Exclusion Act could not apply to him. Wong Kim Ark was free to leave and return as he pleased.

This might seem like a great victory for Chinese Americans, but not everyone was happy with the ruling. Justice John Harlan—the man sometimes upheld today as the great defender of racial justice for his dissent in *Plessy v. Ferguson*—had once again joined the dissent, this time arguing that Chinese people are too foreign to ever belong in the United States. And after the ruling, because of the anti-Chinese racism of the time, Wong Kim Ark was still forced to follow other restrictions that targeted Chinese Americans. For example, he still had to carry documents signed by white people verifying that he was born in the United States. He still had to deal with discrimination in employment and the threat of racial violence. Today, most people believe that Wong Kim Ark eventually did what his parents did to escape discrimination, and that in the end he moved to China to live out the rest of his life.

TODAY, almost all people born in the United States are considered U.S. citizens, regardless of the citizenship status of their parents. The legal right of birthright citizenship is thanks to Wong Kim Ark, born in a small apartment in San Francisco, California, in 1873, and the people of various backgrounds who supported him.

PAPER SONS AND DAUGHTERS

Even though the Chinese Exclusion Act was the law of the land for decades, this law was never able to completely end Chinese immigration to the United States. Wong Kim Ark's court case and the law of birthright citizenship meant that, if a Chinese person could prove that they had been born in the United States or were born to United States citizens, they could not be legally excluded from entering the country. In the years after the Wong Kim Ark decision, these newly proven U.S. citizens were freer to come and go than they had been previously. Others, however, used fake paperwork to gain the same freedoms. These people—who were U.S. citizens on paper only—are sometimes known as "paper sons" and "paper daughters."

On Wednesday, April 18, 1906, a massive earthquake struck the coast of Northern California. At first, San Francisco's Chinatown remained relatively undamaged, but soon fire broke out across the city. Soldiers tried to stop the fire by setting off explosions that would stop its path, but these explosions led to even more fires. By the end of the day on Thursday, Chinatown was rubble and ashes. More than three thousand people lost their lives in the earthquake and fire, which burned for four days. More than 80 percent of San Francisco was destroyed.

Let Us Have No More China-towns in Our Cities

The cities in the immediate vicinity of San Francisco bay never in the past had such opportunity as now to forever do away with the huddling together of Chinese in districts where it is undesirable, from the standpoint of civilization to permit the lower and vicious classes of Orientals to congregate. The opportunity should be promptly seized and vigorously prosecuted to the end that no more Chinatowns should be permitted to exist in San Francisco, Oakland, San Jose, Berkeley, Alameda or other nearly cities and towns.

Chinese were permitted to create a Chinatown in San Francisco. The Orientals were willing to pay high rentals for shacks that few white persons would occupy free of charge. Ultimately as the Chinese engaged in manufacturing and trade, many of them acquired wealth and purchased realty in Chinatown. The fact that they now own land where San Francisco Chinatown stood is being urged in some quarters as a bar to any successful attempt to prevent rebuilding of that plague spot.

Happily the constitution and th'

A headline in the Oakland Enquirer *from April 23, 1906, advocating for the eradication of Chinese American communities.*

Some people saw the earthquake and destruction of Chinatown as an opportunity for exclusion. They argued that the Chinese community should not be allowed to remain and rebuild their homes in America. Others saw an opportunity for more inclusion. Many legal documents, including the birth records of Chinese Americans, had been destroyed in the earthquake and fire. It would be harder for the U.S. and state governments to prove whether a person was or wasn't really born in the United States, because people could simply argue that their records had been destroyed in the earthquake. The paper sons and paper daughters were Chinese people who were not born in the United States but were able to get papers that said they were. Despite the Chinese Exclusion Act, on paper these Chinese Americans would have to be allowed to stay.

There were two main ways that people were able to get these papers saying that they were U.S. citizens. The first was by claiming that they were born in the United States and, because of the Wong Kim Ark case, they were citizens by birth. People who made this argument claimed that they had been born in the U.S. but that their papers were destroyed in the San Francisco earthquake. If nobody could prove otherwise, these people were given new papers affirming their citizenship. This was difficult to prove, however. Often, just like Wong Kim Ark had needed to do, these Chinese Americans needed white people to say that they had been born in the United States. It was difficult to find white people who were willing to risk their own freedom by being accused of lying to support a Chinese person.

The other way that people gained citizenship on paper was more common, and even more complicated. A Chinese American man, one who had already legally proven that he was a citizen of the United States, would go back to visit his family in China. He would then report to the United States that, while in China, he had had a child. This child, by being born to a U.S. citizen, would also have the right to U.S. citizenship. Now, sometimes the man really would have had a child, and that child would eventually come to the United States as a citizen. Other times, the man would have a child but would never plan to bring the child at all. Instead, he would sell the child's paper for a good price to someone else who wanted American citizenship. This person would take on the child's identity to come to the United States as a citizen on paper. And sometimes the man never really had a child at all—he would simply claim that he'd had a child, obtain the document from the U.S. government, and sell the slot anyway! Many Chinese families thought that it would be more useful to buy these documents for their boys than their girls because boys could earn more money in the U.S., and so there were far more paper sons than paper daughters.

Some people might say that what paper sons and paper daughters were doing was wrong and illegal, and some people use this part of history to justify or support the idea that immigrants are criminals. But you can also think of it this way: The Chinese Exclusion Act was a racist and unjust law to begin with. European settlers had come from other parts of the world and taken land from Indigenous Americans. They had forcibly enslaved and transported Black Americans to help build the wealth of the nation. And now they wanted to restrict other people's entry and right to remain in the United States. The origin stories of the United States talk about European immigrants coming to America to find a better future, and now the descendants of these Europeans wanted to arrest Chinese people for doing the same thing. Just like Homer Plessy was arrested for sitting in the white train compartment and Wong Kim Ark was arrested for trying to return to his home country, paper sons and daughters were breaking laws that should never have existed to begin with.

Of course, being allowed to enter the United States wasn't as simple as buying someone's paper in China and walking through the immigration station with the paper in your hand. The U.S. government was suspicious that so many Chinese-looking people were claiming to be U.S. citizens. They must have realized that not everyone who entered the country was who they said they were. The American government decided that they would carefully try to prove someone's identity before allowing that person to enter. In China, people who were trying to enter the U.S. as paper sons or paper daughters would spend weeks or months preparing for the questions that they knew they would face once they arrived in their new country. If they did not answer correctly, the border agents could lock them up and eventually deport them back to China. These hopeful immigrants knew that they had to be prepared for the intense interrogation process that they would face once they arrived at the immigration processing station in the San Francisco Bay, a now infamous place known as Angel Island.

LET'S THINK ABOUT THIS:

1. Why are some groups of immigrants seen as more desirable than other immigrants? Who gets to decide?

2. This chapter describes people like Frederick Douglass and Thomas Riordan who were not Chinese but who stood up for the rights of Chinese Americans. Why is it important to have people from different groups supporting each other's rights? How can you apply this practice to your own life?

3. This chapter describes many laws that were based on racist fears about groups of people, like the Page Act, the Chinese Exclusion Act, and the Geary Act. Can you think of other laws that existed in the past that were unfair or unjust? What about today? What are some ways that people try to change unjust laws?

CHAPTER 6

ANGEL ISLAND

L ike Ellis Island in New York Harbor was the gate of entry to the East Coast of the United States, Angel Island was the gate of entry to the West Coast. In the 1800s, Angel Island became a military fort. Later, a quarantine station was built on the island. If a ship arrived in San Francisco Bay and the border agents thought there might be a disease on board, all the passengers would have to be tested and quarantined at Angel Island. Most of the ships that were quarantined arrived from China, and the stereotype that Chinese people spread diseases only continued to grow. Asian people who were quarantined at Angel Island had to eat in areas segregated from other people, and the island even had a crematorium—a place to cremate the remains of people who died.

In 1910, Angel Island became an immigration station. Everyone who arrived at the Port of San Francisco from another country had to go through the island before being allowed to enter the United States. In the thirty years that the Angel Island Immigration Station was in operation, hundreds of thousands of people from eighty-four different countries went through the station to have their papers and their health checked and proven okay. Many European people were questioned and forced to stay at the island in quarantine, but they were segregated into better housing and ate better food than immigrants from other parts of the world. The main targets of questioning were Asian immigrants, and especially Chinese people who were still facing the legal exclusion of the Chinese Exclusion Act.

Immigrants waiting at Angel Island.

More than 175,000 Chinese immigrants came through Angel Island during those years. Most of these were young men between the ages of fourteen and eighteen, and most had to undergo serious questioning. The white people who worked at Angel Island Immigration Station called the island the "Guardian of the Western Gate." In other words, they felt proud that this island would guard or protect America from "undesirable foreigners" trying to enter from the west. These border agents spent an average of two weeks questioning each Chinese immigrant who came through Angel Island. Many people were turned away, especially the people who were trying to enter the U.S. using papers that were not their own. The border agents would ask difficult questions about the places in China that the person's papers said they were from. These questions might ask about landmarks in their village, like trees and lakes, or the names of shops, or the depth of the village well. Of course, the Chinese immigrants who had purchased someone else's papers often didn't have direct experience of these places. This is why the paper sons and paper daughters spent so long studying before they tried to make the journey. After the interviews, the border agents would check the answers with someone in the United States that the paper claimed was a relative. The answers had to match. If a paper son's or paper daughter's story changed or seemed suspicious, they would be sent back to China and banned from entering the United States in the future. Some Chinese people had to spend far longer than two weeks answering questions. There are even records of people who were detained at Angel Island for almost two years.

Angel Island continued to be the main processing center for Chinese immigrants through the early 1900s. Over the same period, more immigrants arrived from other parts of Asia as well, particularly Japan and South Asia. The border agents who wanted to limit Chinese immigration were similarly unhappy about these other groups, and so they used the same methods of detention and questioning on all Asian immigrants, regardless of what country they were from.

The experience of being detained on Angel Island was lonely and scary. Today, you can visit Angel Island and still see hundreds of poems and other inscriptions that people carved on the walls there. One man, only identified as Lee from Toishan, carved a poem dated September 4, 1911. It roughly translates as:

Sitting alone in the customs office,
How could my heart not ache?

Had my family not been poor,
I would not have traveled far away from home.
It was my elder brother who urged me
To embark on a voyage to this shore.
The black devil here is unjust—
He forces the Chinese to clean the floor.
Two meals a day are provided,
But I wonder, when will I be homeward bound?

From this poem, we can feel Lee's heartbreak. He misses his family, but he feels like he had no choice but to try to enter the United States. The United States was an unfriendly place to Chinese people, but it was also still "Gold Mountain." So many immigrants across American history have weighed the decisions that Lee had to make, ultimately deciding that whatever hardships they might face in the United States would be far less than what they were already experiencing. Lee's family was poor, probably so poor that they were not sure that they would survive. His older brother felt

Poetry etched on the walls of the detention barracks by immigrants detained at Angel Island.

that Lee could earn money in the new country to support his entire family back home. But what Lee found in America was even worse than he might have imagined, and it was certainly not riches nor an easy life. The "black devil" in the poem probably refers to the harsh conditions of Angel Island, rather than a Black person. Instead of finding an easy life in America, Lee found himself sitting alone, forced to clean the floors, to eat only a little, and to miss his family and his home.

Another poem, this one etched into the walls by an unknown author, describes the difficult journey to arrive in the United States:

Originally, I had intended to come to America last year.
Lack of money delayed me until early autumn.
It was on the day that the Weaver Maiden met the Cowherd
That I took passage on the President Lincoln.
I ate wind and tasted waves for more than twenty days.
Fortunately, I arrived safely on the American continent.
I thought I could land in a few days.
How was I to know I would become a prisoner suffering
in the wooden building?
The barbarians' abuse is really difficult to take.
When my family's circumstances stir my emotions,
a double stream of tears flows.

I only wish I can land in San Francisco soon,
Thus sparing me this additional sorrow here.

Angel Island Immigration Station was shut down in 1940 after a fire destroyed the main building. The station was returned to the army, but the island's history with Asian people was not over. During the Second World War, Angel Island was once again used to detain and question Japanese, Korean, and Okinawan people, now taken as prisoners of war.

TYRUS WONG, A CELEBRATED ARTIST

Have you ever seen the movie *Bambi*? Even if you haven't, you can probably picture it in your mind. That picture would not exist if it weren't for a paper son named Tyrus Wong.

If the immigration agents at Angel Island could find no reason to deport a paper son or paper daughter, they would have no choice but to let them enter the United States. In 1910, a child named Wong Gen Yeo was born in Taishan, the same region of Guangdong Province that Wong Kim Ark was from. Wong (or Wang in Mandarin) is a very common Chinese surname, so it is unlikely that they are related. The family had two children, Wong Gen Yeo and his sister, and they were relatively poor. Gen Yeo's parents decided that their son would have a better future in America. When Wong Gen Yeo was ten years old, he and his father left China. Gen Yeo would never see his mother or his sister ever again.

Wong Gen Yeo's father, a man originally named Wong Sy Po, had previously come to America as a paper son. The father's new name—the name that was on his paper—was Look Get. Wong Gen Yeo was also trying to enter the new country as a paper son. His new name would be Look Tai Yow. The Wongs were fortunate to share a first-class room with another passenger on the SS *China,* the ship that took them across the Pacific Ocean. Even though Gen Yeo did not have to travel in steerage, he still got seasick quite a bit on the journey. Gen Yeo spent his time wandering around the decks looking at the other passengers, including people from America, Japan, and of course, many other people from China.

When they finally arrived at Angel Island on December 30, 1920, Wong Gen Yeo and his father were separated for questioning. Gen Yeo's father (going by his paper name Look Get) was allowed to pass through pretty quickly. He'd been through before, so he didn't need to undergo the same intensive questioning as his first entry to the country. The younger Wong Gen Yeo (going by his paper name Look Tai Yow), on the other hand, would have to wait. He was the only child being held at Angel Island at the time, and he was lonely and frightened. Later in life, Gen Yeo would remember how hot it was, how boring it was, how much he missed his family, and how much he cried. He said that Angel Island was "just like jail." At some point, an American guard gave Gen Yeo some chewing gum to comfort him and quiet him down, and the boy spent the next few days passing his time by chewing gum or playing with his gum. On good days he was able to spend time swinging on a swing. On January 27, 1921, Gen Yeo was finally questioned by three immigration agents. The boy had done his homework well, and all of his answers matched the answers his father—now staying in Sacramento, California—had given to immigration agents just nine days beforehand. The agents were satisfied that "Look Tai Yow" really was the son of "Look Get." On January 31, 1921, the agents issued a paper saying that Look Tai Yow was a United States citizen, and they allowed the boy to finally leave Angel Island to join his father in Sacramento.

Wong Gen Yeo's life in Sacramento was difficult, but it also opened up many opportunities for the boy and his family. Gen Yeo and his father shared a small room in a boardinghouse with other Chinese immigrants. They didn't have much privacy, and they even had to share a bathroom with the other boarders. Gen Yeo's father noticed that the boy was very interested in art, and that he had talent, too. The father purchased a brush and taught his son how to paint watercolors and write Chinese calligraphy. The family could rarely afford ink or nice paper, so Wong Gen Yeo usually practiced his art using plain water on newspapers that his father brought home after a long day of work.

Wong Gen Yeo started attending an American school in Sacramento, using his paper son name. There, a teacher decided that "Tai Yow" sounded like "Tyrus," and that Tyrus would be a more appropriate name for a new American. Wong Gen Yeo went by the name Tyrus Wong for the rest of his life. Tyrus didn't much like school, especially after his father took him out of the American school and put him in a Chinese school in Sacramento. The new school was strict and the lessons were long, and all that Tyrus wanted to do was paint. When Tyrus's father had to move to Los Angeles to find work, leaving young Tyrus to live alone at the boardinghouse, the boy began skipping school. His grades rapidly dropped, and he wasn't allowed to pass to the next grade. When Tyrus's father found out, he was furious. He immediately sent for his son to join him in Los Angeles. Once again, Tyrus Wong was moving to an unfamiliar place.

The move to Los Angeles would turn out to be a lucky one for the family, even though they still didn't have much money. The father and son still had to live in a dirty, crowded boardinghouse. The elder Wong worked in a gambling house and even young Tyrus had to work to support the family. He earned fifty cents a day as a houseboy, working after school to clean, run errands, and do other chores and tasks for two families in Southern California. He was still only about twelve or thirteen years old. At his American junior high school, a teacher noticed that Tyrus Wong was a talented artist. The teacher told Tyrus about a place in Los Angeles called the Otis Art Institute and helped arrange for a summer scholarship for the boy. At the art school, Tyrus thrived. He loved it so much that he did not want to return to junior high when the summer program was over. Tyrus's father did not know what to do. On the one hand, he had left his life and family behind in China to help his son have a better life. Here was the opportunity of a lifetime—something that his son both loved and was good at. On the other hand, the Otis Art Institute cost ninety dollars a year, a huge amount of money for the family. How would they ever pay the tuition?

In the end, a father's love for a son won out, and the elder Wong found a way to earn and borrow the money needed for Tyrus to attend art school full-time. Tyrus Wong attended Otis for five years, sometimes working as a custodian at the school to help to pay his fees. Tyrus was a talented artist and a top student, and he eventually earned a full scholarship to continue at Otis. His father must have been so proud. Tyrus finally graduated from Otis in 1932. Sadly, his father died not very long after. Tyrus Wong was on his own once again.

Tyrus Wong worked steadily as an artist throughout the 1930s. He painted beautiful murals on the walls of Chinatown restaurants. He participated in something called the Federal Arts Project, one of President Franklin D. Roosevelt's initiatives during the Great Depression. Tyrus and another Asian American art student from Otis, the Japanese American painter Benji Okubo, founded something they called the Oriental Artist Group of LA, a collective of Asian American artists from the city. This group was famous for their combination of Asian and Western artistic styles and methods. Both Tyrus Wong's name and his art are strong representations of his

Tyrus Wong painting.

Chinese American identity. He didn't have to give up his Chinese identity or experiences to be American. Instead, what it meant to be accepted in America could expand to include someone like Tyrus Wong and the beautiful skills he had to offer.

In 1938, Tyrus Wong got a really big break—a job at the Walt Disney Company. He was hired as something called an "in-betweener," a person who drew the art that created the appearance of movement between the main images of an animation. There were very few Asian employees at Disney, and some of his white colleagues called him names, but they could not deny Tyrus's skill as an artist. Tyrus heard that the studio was trying to make a movie about a deer named Bambi, but the artists were struggling to find a style for the background of the forest. Tyrus saw his opportunity and painted some beautiful landscapes with deer. He used watercolors and pastels, and he combined traditional landscape styles of the Chinese Song Dynasty with more Western styles and techniques. When Walt Disney saw the paintings, he loved them. Tyrus Wong became an important part of the creation of *Bambi,* influencing everything from the colors to the layout to the music. Millions and millions of people around the world have seen and have fallen in love with the beautiful, moody landscapes of *Bambi.*

In 1942, when *Bambi* was finally shared with the public for the first time, Tyrus sadly did not get the recognition he deserved for his work. He had been fired the year before after a workers' strike at Disney, even though Tyrus had not participated in the strike. Tyrus Wong's name only appears near the very end of the credits for *Bambi,* and even though his art influenced the look of the entire movie, his name is only listed as a "background" artist.

After being fired from Disney, Tyrus went to work on many famous movies at Warner Brothers, another movie studio. This time, when workers went on strike, he chose to join them in solidarity. Tyrus ended up spending a night in jail, which he said reminded him of his time at Angel Island. Later on, Tyrus designed greeting cards for Hallmark, painted many paintings, and became well known as a kite maker. Many years after the Walt Disney Company had fired Tyrus Wong and removed most mentions of his name from *Bambi,* they decided to make things right. In 2001, the company named Tyrus Wong a "Disney Legend." Tyrus, then in his nineties, was still alive to receive this great honor. He lived to be 106 years old, and his story and his art have continued to influence generations of artists after him.

• • •

TYRUS WONG LEFT a mark on his country, the United States, in more ways than one. The artist collective he'd created with his friend Benji Okubo was able to create exhibitions of work for American artists with Asian backgrounds. Because of the strong anti-Asian feelings at the time, people like Tyrus and Benji had difficulty convincing many art galleries and museums to display their work. By working together across different Asian nationalities, however, they had a lot more power and influence. Unfortunately, this solidarity was soon torn apart. In the 1940s, as the United States entered war with Japan, discrimination against Japanese Americans reached an all-time high. About 120,000 Japanese Americans, many of them United States citizens, were taken from their homes and incarcerated, or imprisoned. The places these Japanese Americans were incarcerated in are commonly known as internment camps. Benji Okubo was one of these incarcerated Japanese Americans. Many Chinese Americans were worried that they would be mistaken for Japanese and would be beaten by angry Americans or rounded up as well. To avoid this racism, some wore pins on their jackets saying that they were Chinese. Even Tyrus Wong wore one of these pins at times, symbolically distancing himself from people like his old friend Benji.

The solidarity that was being forged between Chinese, Japanese, and other Americans of Asian descent was torn apart by America's fear and hatred. Suddenly, Japanese Americans had found themselves dropped toward the very bottom of the racial hierarchy. Many Chinese Americans, barely holding on to their place in the United States, were terrified that they would be dropped further down as well. The old strategy of divide and conquer that keeps marginalized people apart was alive and well. On top of that, Japan and China were now at war. Even though Tyrus Wong was Chinese *American* and Benji Okubo was Japanese *American,* the tensions between their ancestors' countries made it difficult for old friends like Tyrus and Benji to maintain their solidarity. Still, they had done something very powerful when they had created the Oriental Artist Group of LA. The multiethnic Asian artists' collective that they had started together was a precedent for the later powerful Asian American movements that were to come.

EXCLUDED NO MORE

Tyrus Wong's story is beautiful and inspiring, but it is also unusual. Far more of the paper sons and paper daughters who were allowed to pass through Angel Island had difficult lives. They did not have real papers, so it could be hard to land a job, apply for a loan to buy a house or start a business, or attend college. There was always the possibility that someone would expose them for not being who they said they were, and so they lived under fear of deportation. The end of the Chinese Exclusion Act would take nothing less than a war that consumed most of the world.

On December 7, 1941, the Japanese military bombed the U.S. Navy base at Pearl Harbor, in Hawai'i. Up to that point, the United States had been reluctant to join the Second World War. There were two primary parts of the world where World War II was fought: Europe and the Pacific. The U.S., far away from most of the fighting, wanted to stay out of it. The Germans were working to gain control of Europe, and Japan was working to gain control of the Pacific. Japan had been actively waging war throughout Asia, including violent battles in China, Korea, and down through Southeast Asia into countries like Malaysia (then called Malaya) and the Philippines. The United States, fearful that Japan would eventually control all of Asia, needed to strengthen its alliance with the largest country in East Asia: China.

The U.S. had spent most of the last century doing everything it could to distance itself from China and to exclude Chinese people, but it suddenly needed China and its people in order to win the war. The day after the attack on Pearl Harbor, the United States and China both declared war against Japan. They had both entered the fight, and they were both fighting on the same side.

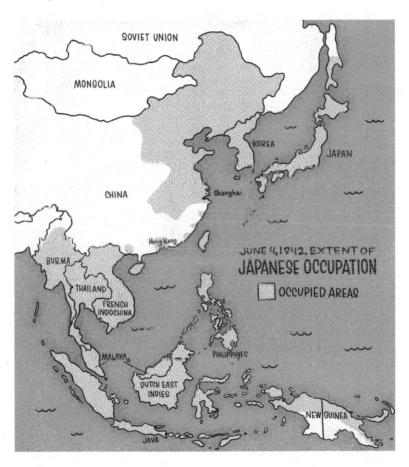

Before World War II, Americans were regularly exposed to anti-Chinese prejudice in the form of *propaganda*, or information that tries to make people believe a certain thing. Newspaper articles pushed for exclusion, political cartoons depicted the racist "John Chinaman" character, and politicians knew they could become more popular by speaking negatively about Chinese people. Now, when the United States government and military needed China to be their allies in the war, all this anti-Chinese sentiment had become a problem. The U.S. government started to produce new kinds of propaganda to change Americans' feelings about China and Chinese people. New movies, posters, and articles depicted righteous Chinese people who were under threat by the evil Japanese. The United States government and other organizations sent food, supplies, and weapons to help China in its fight against Japan, and they encouraged Americans to donate money to

A poster encouraging Americans to support China created by an organization called United China Relief.

join in the effort. Of course, many Americans had spent their whole lives hearing about how dirty, violent, and untrustworthy Chinese people were. If they continued to hold those racist beliefs, they would not feel comfortable about being allies with China or be willing to support Chinese people. The old stereotype of John Chinaman would have to go.

There was another major problem for the United States and China's alliance: the Chinese Exclusion Act. How could the Chinese government trust the United States government when the U.S. had a law saying that Chinese people were not welcome to enter the country? As you know, the Chinese Exclusion Act was based on decades of racial prejudice and discrimination against Chinese people, even Chinese Americans who had been born in the United States. The law would have to change. President Franklin D. Roosevelt wrote to Congress saying that the Chinese Exclusion Act had been a horrible mistake. He said that overturning the law was the only way to win the war. Congress agreed. They drafted something called the Magnuson Act, which would end the Chinese Exclusion Act and, for the first time, allow a very small number of Chinese people to legally immigrate to the United States each year. On December 17, 1943, in the lifetime of many people still living today, President Roosevelt signed the Magnuson Act into law. It took more than half a century, but Chinese exclusion was finally no more.

TOY LEN GOON, AN AMERICAN MOTHER

The old stereotype of dirty, diseased, and dangerous Chinese people in America is sometimes called *yellow peril*. This yellow peril stereotype was behind the John Chinaman caricature and the racist laws that were passed to restrict where he could live, work, and study, whom he could marry, and where he could call home. With the end of the Chinese Exclusion Act, it seemed as if the yellow peril stereotype might go away, but it never really did. You will soon read about how the old yellow peril stereotype has continued to pop up across United States history. But even though this racist stereotype didn't go away entirely, it started to be overshadowed by a very different stereotype, one that is more familiar to people alive today. This stereotype is known as the *model minority myth*.

Propaganda during World War II depicted Chinese people as honest, hardworking, and worthy allies, and many Americans from all different backgrounds started to look more favorably upon Chinese

Americans. Nearly twenty thousand Chinese American men fought for the United States during the war, almost a quarter of all the Chinese men in the country at the time. Some Chinese American women also served during the war. At least one even worked in military intelligence, gathering, translating, and analyzing information to support the war efforts of the United States and its allies. Japanese Americans suffered intense racial prejudice during the war, but Chinese Americans suddenly found themselves higher up on the racial hierarchy. While Japanese American soldiers had to fight in segregated units, most Chinese American soldiers served in units with people from other racial backgrounds, including with white people. Many of the Americans who had previously thought that Chinese people should be kept as perpetual foreigners now had a very different understanding. They saw that Chinese Americans could be loyal to the United States, and they recognized that many Chinese Americans had served their country as war heroes.

There was a history of Chinese Americans serving in the United States military even before the Second World War. In 1917, a man named Dogan Goon left Guangdong Province and arrived in Boston, Massachusetts. (By this time, many Chinese Americans began following the Western tradition of putting the family name last. For the rest of this book, you will mostly see people use their family name as their surname, as is the case with the Goon family.) He

Dogan Goon in military uniform, 1918.

was soon detained and questioned under the Chinese Exclusion Act. Dogan was lucky and was allowed to remain in the country, but he still worried about his future. In order to prove his loyalty to his new country, Dogan Goon joined the United States Army Medical Corps in 1918. Dogan served during a very difficult time. It was the First World War and also the 1918 influenza pandemic, the deadliest pandemic before the Covid-19 pandemic that hit a century later.

In 1919, after losing a limb, Dogan Goon finished his time in the army. He was given United States citizenship in exchange for his honorable service. With citizenship in hand, Dogan settled in Portland, Maine, where he opened a business. Can you guess what kind of business it was? Yes, it was a laundry. A couple of years later, Dogan left a friend in charge of the laundry for a little while so he could travel to China to find a wife. He planned to get married in China, and then bring his new wife back to the United States, where they would start a family as Chinese Americans and as U.S. citizens.

Toy Len Goon arrived in the United States for the first time when she was twenty-nine years old. She was pregnant when she left China. She was nervous about the voyage, and even more nervous about the family she was leaving behind. She worried that her family in China would never escape poverty and that they would starve. But Toy Len Goon was also hopeful that her new country would provide more opportunities for herself, her husband, and their children. Because her husband's citizenship had been gained through military service, the couple had little problem crossing the border into the United States. Toy Len was one of the few Chinese women who were allowed entry into the United States during the period of Chinese exclusion, and it was thanks to the military service of her husband, Dogan. They made their way to Portland, Maine, to resume work in the laundry business that Dogan had started. There were very few Chinese American people in Maine at the time, maybe just one hundred across the whole state. And, like in other states across the country, most of the Chinese Americans in Maine worked in laundry.

Toy Len Goon spent long hours working, sweating over the hot irons and aging her hands in the hot water. She and her husband had eight children. Owning a laundry was hard work, but the family seemed to be prospering in Portland. Then, in 1941, when the eldest Goon child was sixteen and the youngest was only three, tragedy struck. Dogan Goon, the Chinese American war hero, died. Toy Len Goon was left on her own to raise her children and continue the family business.

At first, the city government of Portland did not think that Toy Len Goon would be able to handle her new responsibilities by herself. They tried to convince her to split up her children—eight was a lot for one person to manage, after all—and to place some of them into foster care. Toy Len refused to do this. She had crossed an ocean, leaving behind the family of her birth, to try to create a new life for the children she would raise. She feared that, in foster care, the children would suffer mistreatment or would not be allowed to access opportunities that would help them establish a better future. She did not want her children to have to work long hours of manual labor like she and her husband had done. Their purpose for working in the laundry was to make sure that their children would never have to do such difficult, physical work, and Toy Len was not going to let her husband's death change that.

For the next few years, Toy Len Goon and her children made it work. The siblings helped take care of one another. The older children took time off school to help in the laundry, while the younger children were encouraged to study as hard as they could. Eventually, all the Goon children went on to college or university. They became social workers, engineers, lawyers, doctors, and more—jobs that required higher education and were a far cry from their family's humble roots in the laundry industry. One of the Goon children even earned a Ph.D. Toy Len Goon, in one generation, had achieved the "American Dream."

Some white people who knew Toy Len Goon wanted to share the story of her family's success. A woman named Clara L. Soule worked for the school district in Portland. She ran something called the "Americanization" program. Programs like this focused on helping foreigners assimilate, or become more like white Americans. In some ways, Americanization programs were very helpful. Clara recruited Chinese restaurant workers and other Chinese Americans in Portland to attend classes where they practiced English language skills and learned about topics like civics that would help them to better navigate their life in the United States.

Many Chinese Americans who attended these programs were grateful for the support. There is even a report that the Americanization students in Portland held a grand Lunar New Year feast at a local Chinese restaurant for Clara Soule and her family.

Clara L. Soule, standing in the back of her adult Americanization class. In front of her are students (from left) George Wong, Dan Wong, Henry Wong, Philip Dong, Han Tong, and Chee Wong. All were Chinese American waiters at the Oriental and Empire restaurants in Portland, Maine.

On the other hand, Americanization programs worked under the assumption that to be "American" a person had to act and sound like a white American. This idea of what it means to be American limits the number and types of people who are allowed to feel like they belong in the United States. Instead of expanding the idea of who is American so that the country can be inclusive to all kinds of diverse people, Americanization programs focused on changing anyone who was seen as "different" so that they could be more "acceptable." For example, these programs discouraged new immigrants from speaking their home languages, including within their families. Many Chinese Americans did not teach their own children how to speak their family's dialect, worried that it would hold back their ability to learn English or give them an accent that would make white Americans not accept them. Of course, these children still looked Chinese and were treated as such. Now, however, they did not even have access to their ancestors' language. Many of the children of the Chinese Americans who went through "Americanization" felt doubly isolated. They were not fully American, and they were not fully Chinese. Their parents, only trying to do what was best, ended up sacrificing a major part of who they were.

Clara Soule knew the large Goon family, and she was impressed with Toy Len Goon's progress of Americanization. In just thirty years since arriving in the United States, Toy Len had gone from an anxious young mother to a successful business owner whose children had gone into highly respected, well-paid professions. The Goon family were members of the First Baptist Church in Portland, where the children actively participated in church activities. To someone like Clara Soule, this was the model for how immigrants should behave—Toy Len Goon should be celebrated for what she had done and, perhaps, other Chinese immigrants might learn from her example. Clara nominated Toy Len Goon to become Maine's official mother of the year. The committee was just as impressed by Toy Len as Clara was, and the Chinese-born Toy Len Goon was officially recognized as Maine's ideal mother for the year 1952. Each state's mother of the year was then entered into a selection process for "United States Mother of the Year." In 1952, Maine's nominee won the honor. A committee of reviewers decided that, of all the mothers in the country, Toy Len Goon was the ideal.

In all her years of working in the laundry, Toy Len had only ever taken one week off work. Now she had to leave the laundry behind to receive her award. Toy Len was brought to New York City, where the ceremony was held at the famous and grand Waldorf Astoria Hotel. A lunch was held in her honor, and film crews were there to document the whole affair. Her story was shared in newsreels across the country. Next, Toy Len Goon traveled to Washington, D.C., where she met the First Lady, Bess Truman, and also members of the United States Congress. Toy Len, who didn't feel entirely confident about her English, must have been a little bit bewildered by the whole experience, but she also seemed to be enjoying herself. She smiled broadly for the cameras, and the people she met were impressed by her manners and her composure. The Chinese American community was also proud to see one of their own receive such a special recognition. Chinese Americans in Washington, D.C., New York, and Boston held receptions in Toy Len Goon's honor. In New York City's Chinatown, they even threw a parade.

Toy Len Goon lived to be 101 years old. Today if you visit Portland, Maine, you can see a historical marker in her honor. Toy Len Goon's story was shared all over the United States and beyond. In China and other parts of the world where the overseas Chinese had settled, people saw that America had come a long way since the years of the Chinese Exclusion Act. Toy Len Goon's story suggested that Chinese Americans were welcome after all, and it gave an example of exactly what to do to become successful in the United States. Even though Chinese Americans were still seen as different from white Americans, Toy Len Goon's story suggested that they could become accepted by working hard, joining a church, and prioritizing kids' education over everything. The path to acceptance was to become a "model minority."

Toy Len Goon riding through New York City's Chinatown in a parade celebrating her as Mother of the Year, 1952.

THE MODEL MINORITY MYTH

Toy Len Goon's story is a story of triumph, but the media narrative of the time ignored many important details about her life. One of Toy Len Goon's granddaughters, a professor of anthropology named Dr. Andrea Louie, has been working to better understand and tell a more complete story of her grandmother's life. The common story that was told about Toy Len Goon when she won the Mother of the Year Award focused on her "model minority" characteristics, like politeness, hard work, and fitting into American ideals of motherhood. In reality, Toy Len Goon had to break the mold in order to achieve her success. For example, she had to stand up to the authorities who wanted to separate her children. Even though the media mainly focused on Toy Len's qualities as a mother, she was also a clever businesswoman. She was the one who purchased the building that would hold the family's laundry business and its home. It was rare for women to purchase property or run businesses at the time, and it was even rarer for a Chinese American woman to do so, especially one who did not confidently speak English. But the media focused on Toy Len Goon's "acceptable" qualities instead of her trailblazing ones, and so her story was used to spread and perpetuate the model minority myth, a stereotype that would affect generations of Chinese Americans to come.

We cannot deny the real struggle that Toy Len Goon and her family went through, and the real hard work they put in to achieve greater economic success in their new home. And we also cannot deny how people with power used her story and other stories like it to their own advantage. Toy Len Goon's story was just one story that helped spread the model minority myth across the world. This stereotype is deeply connected to scientific racism, because it claims that Chinese Americans—and many other Asian American groups—are naturally hardworking, talented in subjects like math and science, quiet, and well-behaved. The model minority myth suggested that Chinese Americans are welcome in the United States with open arms, erasing the century of oppression, including physical violence, that had come before. And, of course, Toy Len Goon was only one person. Her experience was not the same as every Chinese American's, but her story was told as if all Chinese Americans are naturally as industrious, resourceful, and accepted by the white American public as she was. One hundred years earlier, Afong Moy had been written about in the press and brought on tour as a strange Chinese woman that the American people might learn from by looking at. It's not hard to see the similarities in Toy Len Goon's experience with being objectified in the press and on tour. In both cases, a Chinese woman was used to illustrate how Americans could or should think about all Chinese people.

Today, you will still see people repeating the stereotypes that are a part of the model minority myth. They often do this to claim that racism and the racial hierarchy are not real. For example, people will say things like "The United States is not racist. Look at how well the Asians are doing! Look at how accepted they are!" You can probably already spot many flaws in this argument. First, not all Asian people are doing well in America. There are some groups of Asian Americans who are economically more successful than the general population, including many Chinese Americans, but this is not true for everyone. For example, you will soon read about how some recent Chinese American immigrants have very different immigration stories from those who were trying to escape poverty in Guangdong Province in the 1800s and early 1900s. Toy Len Goon was given her award in the 1950s, and you know that, up until that point, most Chinese Americans had lived difficult lives. Working on a railroad, on a plantation, or in a laundry is physically demanding and very poorly paid work. At the time that the model minority myth started to take hold, Chinese Americans were by no means a routinely wealthy group.

Second, Asian people were not readily accepted in America. You only need to think about the Los Angeles Chinatown Massacre and the Chinese Exclusion Act to show that the idea that all Chinese people have always been so well accepted is false. Why, then, has this idea become so popular? Many schools today do not tell the stories of violence and exclusion that Chinese Americans experienced. Maybe the people who decide what is taught in school think these stories are not important, or maybe they think that these stories are shameful. But there's another, even more harmful reason that the idea of the "acceptable Asian" has been so frequently repeated and spread: it keeps the racial hierarchy alive.

When someone says "Racism is not real. Look at how well the Asians are doing," they are usually trying to excuse away inequalities experienced by Black, Latine, or Indigenous Americans. In particular, this statement is used to justify anti-Black racism. The statement suggests that Asian Americans, through nothing but hard work and good manners, have been able to pull themselves up from poverty and achieve the American Dream. You can see how someone like Clara Soule would think that Toy Len Goon was the perfect example to help illustrate this idea. But the statement "Racism is not real. Look at how well the Asians are doing" ignores history. It ignores the poverty that many Asian Americans, including Chinese Americans, experienced in the past and even today. It ignores the brutal systems of enslavement, segregation, and other forms of discrimination that Black Americans have experienced for centuries. Many Chinese Americans also began to internalize the model minority myth, believing that they were inherently better or more deserving of a higher place in the racial hierarchy. Of course, most Black Americans and others did not like it when they saw a Chinese American trying to "get ahead" by putting them down. Once again, the model minority myth has been used as a wedge—a tool of the old divide and conquer strategy that keeps communities in competition with one another for power, instead of recognizing that the same forces are keeping these communities from having an equal share of power.

So it's true, Toy Len Goon did prioritize her children's education. But it's also true that she had access to resources (including money and social acceptance) that many Black Americans did not have access to. Saying that Chinese Americans are the "model minority" means that some other groups must not be the "model." In other words, saying that one group is more acceptable than another *by definition* says that there is a hierarchy of race. The model minority myth was used and continues to be used to justify this racial hierarchy, to keep people from marginalized backgrounds divided against each other, and especially to keep Black Americans at the bottom of the social order. And even while being seen as "more acceptable," Chinese Americans were not at the top of the social hierarchy. It doesn't matter that Asian Americans were the "model minority"—even in the name of the stereotype you can see that they were always and forever still a "minority." In other words, they didn't quite belong.

Communism and Capitalism and Democracy

Under communism, individuals do not own land or businesses. Instead, these are owned and controlled by a central authority, usually the government, that redistributes wealth to all people. People who support communism say that it ends class inequalities. People who oppose communism say that it gives too much power to the government, and it unfairly limits difference and disagreement.

Capitalism is an economic system where individuals or companies own and produce wealth, and they operate in competition with one another. People who support capitalism say that it rewards those who are most deserving. People who oppose capitalism say that it gives unfair advantages to those who already hold wealth and power, and it puts more value on money than on people.

Democracy is a system of government run by elected representatives who are voted in by the people.

● ● ●

In spite of all the flaws in the logic behind the model minority myth, it very quickly spread around the world. Toy Len Goon was named American Mother of the Year in the early years of the Cold War. The Cold War is the name given to the time period roughly between the end of World War II and the 1990s. During World War II, one of the United States' allies was the Soviet Union, which later became Russia, Ukraine, and other countries in Eastern Europe and Western Asia. The Soviet Union followed an economic and governmental system called communism, while the United States followed an economic system called capitalism and a system of government called democracy. The countries were able to look past their differences of ideas while they were fighting common enemies during the Second World War, but as soon as the war was over the tensions between them grew. Other countries took sides. Most of the Western European countries and current or former British colonies allied with the United States. This side is referred to as the "Western bloc." Most of the Eastern European countries sided with the Soviet Union. This side is referred to as the "Eastern bloc." Other countries, especially in South America and Africa, managed to stay out of the conflict, at least officially. The Eastern and Western blocs still wanted these countries to choose sides. Whichever side had the most support would have the upper hand.

The Cold War is called "cold" because most of the conflict did not occur with weapons or fighting. Instead, the competing blocs relied on political and economic strategies. One of the main ways that the Cold War was waged was in a battle of propaganda. Writers, filmmakers, and politicians from each side created propaganda to keep the people from their own bloc in line with their side's point of view, and to persuade people from neutral places to pick a side. They also used propaganda to try to get people on the other side to switch allegiances. For example, Soviet propaganda tried to convince Americans to spy on the United States government and to try to take the American system down from the inside. American

COLD WAR
········ ALLIANCES ········

☐ WESTERN BLOC ▦ EASTERN BLOC ☐ NEUTRAL

propaganda tried to do the same thing with people from the Soviet Union.

The United States spread messages all over the world about the dangers of communism, pointing out violent atrocities that had been committed by Soviet leaders like Joseph Stalin. Under Stalin, a million or more Soviet citizens had been put to death, and millions more had starved, been imprisoned, been sent to work in labor camps, or had faced countless other terrible fates. The United States said that communism led to oppressive, dangerous systems, warning that sympathizing with the Soviets was a bad idea. The Soviet Union denied the worst of its atrocities and countered by saying that the United States' claims of being so open, fair, and tolerant were ridiculous. They said that you only had to look at how Black people were treated in the United States to see that the United States wasn't as free as it said it was. The Soviet Union said that the United States' long history of racism was also an oppressive system, warning that sympathizing with the Americans was an equally bad idea.

The United States had a real problem. The Soviet Union was pointing out American racism at a time when Jim Crow was very much alive and well in the United States. Schools, public transportation, and many other parts of American life were still legally segregated by race. The Soviet Union ran stories about violent killings of Black Americans, the murder and forced removal of Native and Indigenous peoples, and the rounding up and imprisonment of Japanese Americans during World War II. With all of this evidence, even the most anti-Soviet person would have a hard time denying that the United States had a racism problem. In order to keep its position as a world power, the United States would urgently need to reject any claims of racism. Chinese Americans would help them make that argument. Remember, one way people use the model minority myth is to say, "Racism is not real. Look at how well the Asians are doing." Stories like Toy Len Goon's were not only used to celebrate one exceptional mother who'd made a home in Portland, Maine. These stories were also used to try to erase centuries of racial oppression in the war of ideas with this new enemy: communism.

COMMUNISM AND CONFESSIONS

The idea of hardworking, successful, and acceptable Chinese Americans spread quickly. It was much nicer for Americans to think of themselves as embracing families like the Goons with open arms, rather than remembering the years of violent oppression and harsh discrimination that had come before (and, in many ways, that still continued). It was also advantageous to use the success of some Chinese Americans to reject any claims that the United States might have a long history of racist laws and beliefs. But there was a problem. The Chinese, like the Soviets, had been an ally of the United States during the Second World War, but as soon as the war was over, China, too, turned toward communism.

The events commonly referred to as the Communist Revolution happened in China in the second half of the 1940s. The revolution, led by a Chinese man named Mao Zedong, radically transformed Chinese society. You might have heard of Mao Zedong as Chairman Mao. As you know, poverty and famine were major issues in many parts of China. Like the United States, China had a deeply rooted social hierarchy, although theirs was based more on social class and ethnicity rather than race. Mao Zedong and his followers claimed that the revolution was going to reset the balance of power in China, giving the people who had always found themselves at the bottom the rights, power, and resources that they deserved. Some overseas Chinese, including some Chinese Americans, were so moved by this message that they returned to China to join in the fight. Supporters of the revolution took land and money away from wealthy people, many of whom were sent to be "reeducated" in labor camps or were even killed. Leaders banned books and speech that disagreed with the ideology of the revolution. Many Chinese people sided with Mao Zedong and the Chinese Communist Party, while other Chinese people supported the Chinese Nationalist Government, led by a man named Chiang Kai-shek. These two sides fought bitterly until Mao Zedong's side defeated the Nationalists. Chiang Kai-shek and his government retreated to Taiwan, which still calls itself the Republic of China, a name that comes from the Chinese Nationalist movement. In October 1949, Mao Zedong declared that China was officially a communist country, now named the People's Republic of China.

China was now the second-largest communist country in the world after the Soviet Union, a major victory for the Eastern bloc. Many Chinese Americans who had left China before the Communist Revolution felt disconnected from the changes that were happening in the country of their ancestors. Today, one of the major differences between groups of Chinese Americans is whether they emigrated from China before or after the Cultural Revolution, a tumultuous phase of Mao Zedong's rule that began in 1966. Most Chinese Americans saw the United States as a land of opportunity. They saw how the younger generation of Chinese Americans, like the children of the Goon family, had far more chances to become economically and socially successful than they had back in China. These Chinese Americans were distrustful of Mao Zedong's words. Many felt upset or unhappy about the more extreme aspects of the Cultural Revolution. During the Cultural Revolution, supporters of Mao Zedong destroyed books and works of art, banned traditions and religions that Chinese people had practiced for centuries, and imprisoned or murdered people who did not agree. Some Chinese Americans even lost relatives in the violence. Today, scholars estimate that more than one million people died during the Cultural Revolution.

There were also some Chinese Americans who supported the revolution. After all, most Chinese Americans had left impoverished parts of China, so many of them found Mao Zedong's message about equality and rights for the people to be powerful. Many of them didn't know about the more violent, brutal aspects of the Cultural Revolution, and others did not care. Many Chinese Americans, especially the older generations, did not read English. They still relied on Chinese-language newspapers for their information, and most of these publications were linked to the Chinese press. Through the Chinese newspapers, communist propaganda spread to Chinese people across the world, including the Chinese American community.

The United States government was in a complicated position. On the one hand, Americans had started to view Chinese Americans as a "model minority." Many Chinese Americans had served honorably in the Second World War, and the propaganda about hardworking, educated, and loyal Chinese Americans had been effective. Unlike during the time of the Chinese Exclusion Act, there now was popular support to make the United States a more welcoming place for them. On the other hand, the United States was worried that Chinese Americans might be more loyal to the Chinese Communist Party than to their American government. They worried that Chinese Americans might act as spies for the Communist Party or spread communist beliefs and literature within the United States. This tension between welcoming more Chinese Americans while at the same time mistrusting their loyalty led to a confessions program.

• • •

BY THE COLD WAR ERA, officials in the United States government realized that many Chinese Americans had entered the country as paper sons and paper daughters. These people had been allowed into the U.S. under a false identity, and so they were not actually legally allowed to be there. The government worried that, if Chinese Americans continued to come to the United States as paper sons and paper daughters, it would be very easy for communist spies to enter the country. All they would have to do is purchase the paper, practice for their interview, and enter the United States under a new name. The United States wanted to keep these Chinese communists out of the country, but there were also many Chinese Americans who had come as paper sons or paper daughters who were not communists at all. Many paper sons and paper daughters, like Tyrus Wong, had not spied on the United States but had instead shared their energies and talents with the country. How could the government address this issue?

In 1956, the United States government started something called the Chinese Confession Program. The idea behind this program was to end the practice of paper sons and paper daughters by correctly identifying the Chinese Americans who were already in the country. The program was also an effort to get Chinese Americans to inform, or to tell on, people who they knew or thought might be communist spies. The government told people in Chinese American communities that if they came forward about their false papers—if they confessed—then they would be given legal status to stay in the United States under their real name. In order for this program to work, the American government had to acknowledge that the Chinese Exclusion Act had been a racist, unfair law. The government had to acknowledge that the Chinese people who had come as paper sons or paper daughters were not illegal criminals, because the law they had broken should never have existed in the first place.

More than ten thousand Chinese Americans willingly confessed during the program, but far more were forced to confess because other people shared their names with the government. Many Chinese Americans treated the program with suspicion and did not trust the promises that the government had made. Some people, trying to secure their American citizenship, turned others in as communist spies, whether or not the other people really were communists. In general, the confession program created mistrust and division within the Chinese American community. It is estimated that only about 13 percent of Chinese Americans participated in the confession program, either willingly or unwillingly. Today, many scholars describe the confession program as dishonest because its main goal was about stopping communism rather than helping Chinese Americans gain real citizenship. Many of the paper sons and paper daughters who didn't participate in the confession program took their real names to their graves, never sharing their true history and background with their children or children's children.

The Chinese Confession Program finally ended in 1966, soon after a new law was passed that would completely change Chinese immigration to the United States. The Immigration and Nationality Act of 1965 opened up legal immigration to far more people. Today, most Chinese Americans have roots in the country that come after 1965. With the passage of this new law, the period of complete exclusion was officially over.

LET'S THINK ABOUT THIS:

1. How might passing through Angel Island change the way immigrants viewed America?

2. Propaganda is still used today in many ways to influence the way people think. What are some examples you've seen?

3. Some people say the model minority myth isn't a bad thing, because it's a "good" stereotype. Is there such a thing as a good stereotype? Why or why not? How can stereotypes that seem good on the surface harm people from that group and from other groups?

CHAPTER 7

BELONGING

Wherever there has been exclusion, there have also been people who have fought for belonging: Ho Ah Kow, whose lawsuit ended the racist practice of cutting off queues. The Chinese railroad workers and multiracial sugar plantation workers, who came together in solidarity to fight for better working conditions and fairer treatment for all. Frederick Douglass, who spoke out for the rights of all people, not just people from one's own groups. Wong Kim Ark, whose experiences and legal battles made birthright citizenship the law of the land. All of these people used the power available to them—whether that was the court system, their platform, or collective power—to try to make a difference. This book will come back to talking about the Immigration and Nationality Act soon, but first it will linger just a bit longer on people who fought for belonging and talk about two Chinese American women who worked to increase representation and belonging in the years before 1965.

ANNA MAY WONG

In 1905, a baby named Wong Liu Tsong was born in Chinatown in Los Angeles, California. Her family gave her the English name Anna May, and the name Anna May Wong would eventually become famous across the world. In a story that is probably familiar to you by now, Anna May Wong's grandfather had come to the United States from Taishan during the Gold Rush, and her American-born father had eventually opened a laundry business. Anna May and her older sister briefly attended their neighborhood public school, but they experienced painful bullying because they were Chinese. Their parents eventually moved them to a missionary school for Chinese students in Los Angeles Chinatown, while the family moved to a new home not too far away. Young Anna May Wong spent her time going to school and helping in the family's laundry. One of her favorite tasks was getting to help deliver the cleaned clothes. She could earn tips doing this, and with those tips she could do what she really liked most—going to the movies. In the early 1900s, movie production moved from New York out to California, and Anna May Wong was growing up right alongside the American film industry.

Anna May's father did not like how obsessed his daughter was with the movies, but he could not stop her. Sometimes she would even skip school to go to the movies, and if her father found out, he would spank her with a bamboo switch. This didn't do anything to stop her interest. Not only did Anna May go to the theater as often as she could, she would also hang around locations where movies were being filmed. Sometimes movies were made in nearby Chinatown, and Anna May would head there from her home to watch the filming in action. Never shy, when she was about nine years old she started talking with the filmmakers she met, begging them for parts in their movies. In 1919, she scored her first role as an extra in a film called *The Red Lantern*. A friend of her father's, without telling him, helped her secure the part. It would take two more years before young Anna May Wong would see her name credited in a movie, but she was already on her way to stardom.

Anna May Wong eventually appeared in more than sixty movies and was the first Chinese American movie star. Her career spanned the early years of Hollywood, and she appeared in both silent movies and full-color features. She also appeared in stage plays and, later, on television. Many early American films included Chinese stories or characters, partly because the film industry was rooted in California, where most Chinese American people lived at the time, partly because Americans had been fascinated by China and Chinese people from the days of Afong Moy, and partly because Chinese people and their stories have always been a part of America and American stories. Because of this, Anna May Wong was often the first choice when filmmakers and studios wanted an Asian actor to play the role of an Asian person. You would think that this would mean that she had many starring roles, but it was quite the opposite. Filmmakers and studios usually preferred having white actors play the roles of Asian people, especially if they were trying to make a movie that would become a big hit.

You might have heard of *blackface,* the practice of white performers covering their faces in black makeup to act as racist caricatures of Black people. Blackface was used in mainstream theater and films well into the mid-1900s. Today, many people find images of blackface performances shocking because they are so exaggerated, offensive, and degrading, but blackface was widespread and common for decades. Just because something is common does not mean that it is right. Blackface was harmful and hurtful for many reasons, including that it introduced or deepened racist beliefs about Black people to huge audiences. Just like the practice of blackface spread racist stereotypes about Black Americans, the practice of *yellowface* spread racist stereotypes about Asian Americans. Both blackface and yellowface were performed onstage long before the invention of film, but the new medium allowed for these racist depictions to reach much wider and entirely new audiences.

Katharine Hepburn in yellowface in the movie Dragon Seed, *1944.*

Throughout Anna May Wong's career, she was overlooked for roles that were given to white people instead. When white actors wore yellowface, they would often wear prosthetics or makeup to make their eyes look slanted, to darken their skin, and to exaggerate their other features. They would speak with a fake accent, sometimes to mock the way Asian people spoke if English wasn't their first language, other times to make sure the audience recognized that the character they were playing was "different." Anna May Wong was praised for her skills as an actor and for her beauty on the screen, but she was rarely allowed to be the star. For one thing, film studios worried that nobody would show up to a movie starring an Asian person. For another thing, it was against the law to show two people from different races kissing on film, just like it was against the law in most places for two people from different races to get married. Even if there was no kiss, studio owners were reluctant to put stars of different races on-screen together, for fear that it would scandalize the white audiences who were their main targets.

So Anna May Wong was often relegated to the supporting role or that of the villain. In 1928, Anna May left Hollywood for Europe, where she felt that she would have greater acceptance and opportunities. She was not the only American of color who felt that Europe was a more accepting place. Some Black soldiers who had been stationed in Europe during the First World War had a difficult time transitioning back to the extreme racism of the U.S. once they'd returned home. Just a few years before Anna May Wong left for Europe, the Black American actress Josephine Baker had left for Paris, and there she became a superstar. Anna May found that she was treated as a star in Germany and in the United Kingdom. She appreciated this recognition, but Hollywood was still the center of the film industry, and in 1930 she returned to California. Over the rest of her career, Anna May would repeatedly be frustrated and turned away from starring roles in the films that she had loved so deeply her whole life.

Anna May Wong experienced racism from Hollywood, and she also experienced sharp criticism from Chinese Americans and Chinese people in China. The roles she was allowed to play often perpetuated anti-Chinese stereotypes, like the cunning, evil woman or the beautiful, young seductress. Many Chinese people criticized the roles that she played, and they criticized her for being a single woman. When Anna May visited China in 1936, she was stopped by protestors from visiting her family's ancestral village. Many Chinese Americans thought that she was an embarrassment whose work only perpetuated harmful stereotypes about Asian people. She did not fit the idea of who a good Chinese American woman should be, and so most of her romantic relationships were with white men. At several points in her life, she almost married, but it was illegal in California. Just like Anna May Wong was barred from loving a white man on-screen, she was legally barred from marrying a white man she loved in real life. There's a story that one of her actor boyfriends offered to marry her in Mexico, where it would have been legal, but when people in the film industry found out, they threatened to ruin his Hollywood career over it, and so the couple broke up. Anna May Wong died in 1961 of a heart attack related to a liver condition.

Although Anna May Wong's story can be painful to learn about, it's important to know that she never simply accepted racism. She spoke out about how filmmakers preferred to cast white American, European, and Latin American actors in roles that were written as Asian characters. She also spoke out about the stereotypes that were associated with Asian characters. For a magazine interview in 1933, she said, "I was so tired of the parts I had to play. Why is it that the screen Chinese is nearly always the villain of the piece, and so cruel a villain—murderous, treacherous, a snake in the grass. We are not like that. How should we be, with a civilization that's so many times older than that of the West. We have our own virtues.

We have our rigid code of behavior, of honor. Why do they never show these on the screen? Why should we always scheme, rob, kill?"

Roles for Asian characters in film and television have continued to be given to white actors, including within your lifetime, dear reader. Today, more and more people are speaking up against this practice, and it is finally starting to change. In the late 2010s, more mainstream movies starring Asian actors playing Asian people were released, proving that filmmakers and studios don't need to use white actors to gain an audience. Today, Anna May Wong is seen as an icon and a trailblazer. In the face of extreme prejudice and discrimination, she showed the world that Chinese American women are here, are skillful, and are powerful. In 2022, Anna May Wong's face appeared on a U.S. quarter, the first time an Asian American person was featured on American currency. Anna May Wong showed the world that Chinese Americans can, and should, belong. Today, film and television representations of Chinese American people are becoming

The Anna May Wong quarter produced in 2022.

more complicated, nuanced, and realistic, promoting greater awareness about Chinese Americans throughout the United States and the world.

Breakfast at Tiffany's

One of the most famous examples of yellowface is Mickey Rooney's portrayal of the Japanese American character Mr. Yunioshi in the film *Breakfast at Tiffany's*. Rooney, a white actor, wore prosthetic teeth and had his eyes taped into slants to play the role. Today, critics are nearly unanimous in calling the role racist and offensive. Even so, the film *Breakfast at Tiffany's* continues to be widely viewed.

MABEL PING-HUA LEE

Anna May Wong's name became famous across the world, and her fame helped to open representation and belonging for more Chinese Americans. Other people have fought for representation and belonging in other ways. Their names may be less famous than the name Anna May Wong, but it is often the people with names we don't know so well who have fought for the greatest positive change.

Mabel Ping-Hua Lee (born as Lee Ping Hua) was born in Guangzhou in 1896. Her father was a Christian minister, and soon after Mabel's birth he

A photograph of Mabel Ping-Hua Lee taken sometime between 1920 and 1925.

left China for Washington State to serve as a missionary to the Chinese American community there. This was during the years of the Chinese Exclusion Act, but because Mabel's father was a Baptist minister, he was granted one of the few exceptions to exclusion. Mabel and her mother had to remain in China. In her early years Mabel attended a missionary school in Guangzhou, where she learned English. Mabel worked hard in school and won the Boxer Indemnity Scholarship, which sponsored Chinese students to be educated in the United States. In 1905, she and her mother also arrived in the United States, where they were reunited with Mabel's father. The family had been allowed to legally enter and settle in the U.S. They had not, however, been allowed to become citizens.

The Lee family made a home in New York City's Chinatown, and Mabel attended a public school called Erasmus Hall that mostly served the city's diverse, and growing, population of immigrant children. Here, she interacted with students from many different racial and ethnic backgrounds. Most of the families, like Mabel's own, had to struggle to make a living. It was here that Mabel became committed to social justice because she realized that many policies and structures of the United States were not fair for all people. In her daily life, she experienced the effects of racism, classism, and other discriminatory systems. The system that she most wanted to change was sexism.

By the time she was sixteen years old, Mabel Ping-Hua Lee was a well-known figure in women's rights circles in New York City. This was 1912, and American women had never had the legal right to vote, also known as *suffrage*. Mabel saw this as a great injustice, and she wanted to do something about it. The Qing Dynasty had recently ended in China, and women's rights were on the rise there as well. Mabel supported social justice and women's rights in both countries— the one she had recently left and the one she now called home.

Alongside her parents and a few other women from Chinatown, Mabel had met with some famous white *suffragists* at a Chinese restaurant. A suffragist is someone who believes in expanding the right to vote. The Chinese Americans who went to the meeting believed that women's rights were important. They hoped that, if they helped stand up for women's rights to vote, the white suffragists would also stand up for Chinese Americans' rights. Mabel spoke to the group about how she experienced both racial and gender discrimination, and she called for better educational opportunities for young Chinese Americans in New York's schools. The suffragists were impressed, and they invited Mabel to participate in an upcoming march.

On May 4, Mabel Ping-Hua Lee rode on horseback at the front of a march for women's suffrage through Greenwich Village in New York City. More than ten thousand people of various ethnic and racial backgrounds marched behind her. Later that year, still sixteen years old, Mabel enrolled at Barnard College, a women's college associated with Columbia

University. She joined the Chinese Students' Association and published essays promoting women's education and voting rights. She gave speeches about these issues to audiences in Chinatown, and some of these speeches were covered by major publications like the *New York Times*. Mabel used the platforms she had available to her—including newsletters, speaking events, and the press—to promote the ideals of justice that she so firmly held. She also understood the need to organize both within one's community, such as by joining the Chinese Students' Association, and with other communities, such as by joining in marches and events with women from other racial backgrounds to fight for voting rights for all.

Suffragists displaying banners before a march through Greenwich Village in 1912.

In 1917, New York State finally granted women the right to vote. In 1920, the Nineteenth Amendment to the Constitution granted women the right to vote across the United States. Mabel Ping-Hua Lee and so many others had advocated long and hard for these rights, and the passage of these laws changed American history forever. Unfortunately, Mabel herself was not allowed to vote. Chinese Americans like her had fewer rights when it came to gaining citizenship—remember, these were still the days of the Chinese Exclusion Act—and without citizenship they also didn't have the right to vote. Though Mabel and many other Chinese Americans had added their voices to the calls for women's rights, most of the white suffragists they had worked with did not hold up their end to fight equally hard to end the Chinese Exclusion Act or to advocate for other rights of Chinese Americans. Mabel was not a United States citizen, and there were very few opportunities for her to become one. She hadn't been born in the U.S., so the birthright citizenship granted by Wong Kim Ark's case did not apply to her. She was a woman, so she couldn't serve in the army and gain citizenship the way Toy Len Goon's husband, Dogan Goon, had done. She could potentially have become a citizen by marriage to a United States citizen, but she didn't marry a Chinese

American man and interracial marriage was uncommon. New York was one of the few states that never officially banned interracial marriage, but she never did get married at all. Today we don't know whether Mabel ever became a United States citizen and gained the right to vote for which she had so fiercely fought.

Mabel Ping-Hua Lee remained an activist and a trailblazer. She went on to earn a master's in education from Teachers College, a progressive school of education also associated with Columbia University. And, in 1921, Mabel graduated from Columbia with a Ph.D. in economics, a rare accomplishment for a woman at that time, and even rarer for a Chinese American woman. Her plan had been to leave the United States after graduating to return to China and open a girls' school, but when her father died in 1924, she decided to stay in New York. She began working at his former church, the First Chinese Baptist Church, and eventually opened a community center to provide resources, health care, childcare, and classes for New York's Chinese American community. Mabel Ping-Hua Lee might never have been able to vote or experience the rights of a full U.S. citizen, but she dedicated her life to ensuring that the next generation would have more rights and access to opportunities than the generation that came before. Today, if you are in New York's Chinatown and you need to buy some stamps or deliver a package, you can do so at the Mabel Lee Memorial Post Office, named in her honor.

THE IMMIGRATION AND NATIONALITY ACT

Up to this point in this book, almost every Chinese American story you've read has had its starting point in Guangdong Province in southern China. All of that would change with the passage of the Immigration and Nationality Act of 1965. In the decades before 1965, the *quota* system for immigration put a strict limit on how many people could immigrate to the United States from various countries. These quotas strongly favored European and other white immigrants while severely limiting Black, Asian, and other immigrants of color. During the Civil Rights Movement of the 1960s, more and more people started speaking out against the quota system. Members of Congress who agreed that the quota system was unjust introduced a bill to try to create a fairer immigration system. It took several years for this bill to be signed into law, however. Many Americans, including some influential members of Congress, opposed opening immigration to more people. They worried that changing the immigration laws would make America a less white and less Christian nation. But in the end, enough lawmakers decided that the Immigration and Nationality Act was an important step toward justice. On October 3, 1965, President Lyndon B. Johnson signed the Immigration and Nationality Act into law.

The new law immediately changed immigration to the United States. During the thirty years before 1965, about six million people legally immigrated to the country. During the thirty years following 1965, the number was eighteen million people. In the 1950s, most legal immigrants came to the United States from Europe. Only 6 percent came from Asia, and an even smaller proportion of that number came from China specifically. After the new law passed, the numbers shifted a lot, and European immigrants became the minority. By the 1990s, it was clear that the Immigration and Nationality Act had in fact changed the racial makeup of the United States. Some people, like the lawmakers who tried to block the law from passing, were upset about white people losing their clear majorities and wanted the country to bring back exclusion laws. Other people thought it was good for America to be more inclusive. They believed that

America could welcome people from all over the world, regardless of their language, religion, or race.

In the first few years of the Immigration and Nationality Act, some of the most significant increases in immigration came from Southeast Asia. The United States was engaged in violent war efforts in the region, displacing millions of people. The war in Southeast Asia is often called the "Vietnam War." The war affected people in Cambodia and Laos as well as Vietnam. Hundreds of thousands of Southeast Asian refugees, who would previously have been excluded, made their way to the United States to try to build a new life. As the years went by, immigration from across the rest of Asia also increased, including from South Asia, Central Asia, and East Asia. Most Asian American people in the United States today come from families that moved to the country after 1965. The new law significantly changed the numbers of Asian Americans in the country, and it significantly affected how other Americans thought about and interacted with Asian Americans. These shifts also affected Chinese Americans.

Most Chinese Americans who came to the United States before 1965 arrived as laborers. They usually came from poor or working-class backgrounds and did not have much education. When they first arrived in the United States, they tended to work difficult jobs in unpleasant conditions. The most fortunate families used education to help their children move into the American middle classes. After 1965, the "typical" Chinese American immigrant started to shift away from physical labor to highly educated professions. The new immigration law put a preference on immigrants who could work in medicine, science, and engineering—jobs that were rapidly creating wealth for America in the second half of the 1900s. These jobs typically require that workers have a higher education degree, and people with higher education degrees are more likely to come from middle- or upper-class backgrounds than working-class ones. Newer Chinese American immigrants therefore tended to come from higher social class backgrounds than the Chinese American immigrants who'd come before them. Not all recent Chinese American immigrants matched this description, but enough did that people's ideas about Chinese Americans as a whole started to change.

The model minority myth, which had taken root in the 1940s and 1950s, became much more widespread as the idea of the "typical" Chinese American immigrant started to shift as well. The Immigration and Nationality Act meant that America was creating space for the highest skilled and highest educated people from China to immigrate to the United States. In other words, the laws were actively making it easiest for people who fit the stereotypes of the "model minority" to immigrate. For example, people who believe in the model minority myth will sometimes say things like "Asian people are naturally good at math." Well, the immigration law made it easier for Asian immigrants who had studied mathematics to enter the country than immigrants with other backgrounds. It's not that Asian people are born being better at math than other people, it's that the laws brought in more Asian people who had math degrees.

The new immigration laws also put a preference on families staying together. Chinese Americans who already called America home were able to help family members in other places to immigrate to the United States as well. It also became easier for whole families to immigrate. These newer families again tended to come from higher education, and thus higher class, backgrounds than the earlier Chinese Americans. Highly educated parents tend to raise highly educated children, so the model minority stereotype extended from generation to generation.

You've already read about the harm that the model minority myth has caused to Asian communities,

Black communities, and other communities of color, but many newer Chinese American immigrants embraced this model minority stereotype. After all, who wouldn't want to be seen as the best? The true history of Chinese Americans before this point was almost never taught in school, so many newer immigrants didn't know anything about the violence and racism that Chinese Americans had experienced for so many years. Instead, these newer immigrants only saw images depicting Asian Americans as welcome, exceptional, and accepted. In many ways, the model minority myth was its own type of propaganda, working as a *recruitment strategy* for the American Dream. This means that the stereotype helped to spread the idea that America is a place free from discrimination and where anyone can succeed, usually in terms of making money. People from around the world have continued to come in pursuit of that American Dream. Some immigrants have found the belonging and success they were looking for, and some have not. The journey has always been a lot more complicated than the stereotypes would suggest.

Unfortunately, believing in the model minority myth also means believing that other groups are not the "model," or are not as good or as worthy. Today, younger Chinese Americans and other Asian

Americans are far more likely to reject and speak out against the model minority myth than their parents' generations were. Today, people are learning or relearning the true histories of these groups and are taking a stand together to try to dismantle stereotypes and racism of all kinds.

BECOMING ASIAN AMERICAN

You've seen the term "Asian American" a few times throughout this book, and it's probably a familiar term to you. Today, we use the term Asian American to mean any American who has family ancestry in Asia. But Asian American is a pretty new term compared to the history of the United States. Most people trace this term to 1968 and students in Berkeley, California, who believed that solidarity was the only path to justice.

The 1960s was an era of great social change. People from many different racial, religious, and other backgrounds were organizing together to demand justice. The term Asian American is usually attributed to graduate students named Emma Gec and Yuji Ichioka, who brought American students with ancestry across East and Southeast Asia together to form the Asian American Political Alliance. Like the multiracial coalition of plantation workers in Hawai'i, these diverse Asian American students realized that they could gain more attention for their cause and make more positive change by joining together than by operating separately. The students learned a lot about organizing and solidarity from the Black freedom movement and the anti-war movement of the 1960s, and they decided to apply those lessons to advancing the rights of Asian Americans as well.

The Asian American student activists had family backgrounds from China, Japan, Korea, the Philippines, and other countries, many of which had decades or centuries of conflict between one another. It was only two decades earlier that China and Japan had been at war and the Chinese American Tyrus Wong had distanced himself from Japanese Americans like his old friend Benji Okubo. The student activists did not ignore the historical conflicts between their ancestors' countries, but they realized that most Americans did not see these differences and distinctions. The students knew that there was something similar about how they were all seen and treated in the United States. Gordon Lee, who embraced the term Asian American in the 1960s, wrote in 2003, "This new identity arose out of our common experiences in America, the experience of being treated as if we were all the same and of an inferior race. As a result, the differences in our home countries became less important and we were able to find a common interest and identity with each other."

The term Asian American is complicated. It can sometimes erase just how diverse this group of people really is. Some people say that the term suggests that Asian Americans are a *monolith,* or a group where everyone is essentially the same. When most Americans think of this term, they think of East Asian people, and particularly the groups of East Asian Americans who have come to the United States from higher education backgrounds since 1965. In other words, this term is associated with the model minority myth. Of course, Asia is a lot more diverse than that. You've read many stories about East Asian people, like Chinese Americans, who have been in the United States for generations, who have had to work dangerous physical jobs, or who have experienced extreme prejudice and racism. You've read about Japanese Americans who were incarcerated in internment camps or forced to work on sugar plantations for meager wages. You've read about Southeast Asians who came to the United States as refugees, often because of American war efforts in their home countries. There are also so many stories of people from South Asia, Western Asia, Central Asia, and other parts of the region that could fill up whole books of their own. The "Asian

American" identity umbrella is large and diverse, and people who identify as Asian American have a wide range of histories, stories, experiences, beliefs, practices, and more.

You might have seen terms like Asian Pacific American (APA); Asian American Pacific Islander (AAPI); Asian, Pacific Islander, and Desi America (APIDA); and so many more. These terms are created to be more inclusive of people from the Pacific Islands or from South Asia. Throughout the rest of this book, you will most often read the abbreviation AAPI, but some people prefer to use other acronyms. Like Asian American, these terms often erase the experiences of people from the most marginalized groups and instead applies the model minority myth to all people of Asian descent, regardless of their real experiences. For example, the model minority myth centers on the success of some East Asian and South Asian groups and hides the struggles of many Southeast Asian, Pacific Islander, and other AAPI groups. In 2020, the average Chinese American woman earned $1.00, and the average Taiwanese American woman earned $1.21 for every dollar that the average white man made in the United States. This would suggest that Asian American women no longer face oppression or marginalization in the country. Remember, though, that most Chinese Americans now in the

U.S. came after 1965 and were more likely to come from higher income and higher social class backgrounds than previous generations. Also in 2020, the average Fijian woman earned 55 cents for that same dollar, and the average Nepalese woman earned only 50 cents. The model minority myth makes it harder to advocate for fairer wages for these groups, because the more economically successful groups raise the average salary of "Asian American women" as a whole.

The MODEL MINORITY MYTH and the PAY GAP between AAPI WOMEN

2020 MEDIAN EARNINGS OF FULL-TIME, YEAR-ROUND WORKERS

WHITE, NON-HISPANIC MEN ($1)

NEPALESE WOMEN	$0.50
FIJIAN WOMEN	$0.55
CHINESE AMERICAN WOMEN	$1
TAIWANESE AMERICAN WOMEN	$1.21

Today, the movement to *disaggregate* data, or to report data that doesn't lump all Asian American or AAPI people in a single group, is an important step to changing this erasure. You can help to support this movement by advocating for data disaggregation at your school. You can also help by using specific language when you talk about different Asian American or AAPI people. When you are talking about all Asian Americans, it's okay to say Asian American, but if you are only talking about East Asian Americans, say East Asian American. When you are talking specifically about Chinese Americans, say Chinese Americans. These practices can help people understand that not all Asian American people are the same.

While umbrella terms like Asian American can create problems, they are also very powerful. There is no need to get rid of these terms completely; we just need to recognize when and how to use them. Many people describe Asian American as a "political identity." This does not mean that it is about a specific political party. It means that the term has to do with power and how people work together to affect society. Some Chinese Americans will identify both by the political identities of Asian American or AAPI *and* by a more specific ethnic identity, like Chinese American. Some will also identify by an even more specific Chinese ethnicity like Cantonese, Hokkien, or Teochew. All people have multiple identities, and these examples show us that it is possible to hold on to our individual and group identities at the same time that we hold broader political identities that help us to advance rights for all people. The student activists of the 1960s knew that a collective identity helped them build collective power, regardless of what specific ethnicities they held. Perhaps one of the most important moments for the Asian American movement came in the 1980s after the tragic murder of a Chinese American man named Vincent Chin.

VINCENT CHIN AND THE ASIAN AMERICAN MOVEMENT

Vincent Chin was born in Guangdong Province in 1955, where he spent his earliest years in an orphanage. He was adopted by a Chinese American couple, Bing Hing "David" and Lily Chin, and brought to the United States in 1961. Bing Hing Chin had come to the United States as a young man, served in the Second World War, and gained his citizenship. He returned to China to marry Lily, and the couple settled in the United States to start a family and build a life together. Lily Chin's great-grandfather had been part of the early waves of Chinese laborers who came to California in search of gold. Not finding any, he had ended up working on the railroads, risking his life as he built tunnels through solid rock. His family eventually returned to China, but now it was Lily making the journey across the Pacific Ocean to find a better life. Like so many Chinese Americans, the Chin family worked in a basement laundry. They worked hard hoping for a better future for Vincent, their only child, who was outgoing and fun-loving. The family lived in Highland Park, Michigan, a city that is inside the larger city of Detroit. When Vincent was growing up, Detroit was the heart of the American car industry. By 1950, almost two million people lived in the city and its surrounding areas, many of whom had come to work in the auto industry. When Vincent was a child, however, the city rapidly changed. Many Black Americans had left the racism of the Jim Crow South to try to find better lives in the Midwest, including in Detroit. Manufacturing jobs did not require a higher education, and they paid well. Immigrants from around the world also came to Detroit in search of work.

Many of the city's white residents did not like that so many people of color were settling in the area. By the 1960s, Detroit's car manufacturers were already starting to shut down operations in the city, moving to the suburbs or other places where it would be cheaper to run a car plant or where they could pay lower wages to their employees. Jobs were becoming scarcer, and many white working people blamed the newer arrivals. Instead of blaming the car companies for moving jobs away, they turned their frustration against working people of color, particularly Black Americans. The old forces of divide and conquer were once again alive and well.

In many Detroit neighborhoods, Black Americans had no choice but to live in run-down, cramped apartments. They were turned away from purchasing homes or renting in better conditions, while many white residents moved to the suburbs to avoid living in mixed-race neighborhoods. Most Detroit police officers were white, and many Black residents felt that the police unfairly wielded their power in Black neighborhoods. Black residents were far more likely than white residents to be turned away from jobs, to be underpaid even if they were employed, and to have poor access to housing, health care, and education. Distrust between the city's Black and white communities continued to grow. In 1967, the distrust transformed into violence.

The Detroit Rebellion, sometimes known as the Detroit Riot or the 12th Street Riot, lasted for five days. White police raided a Black-owned bar that was operating without the proper licenses, where eighty-two people were celebrating the return of two men who had come home from serving in the war in Southeast Asia. The police arrested everyone, and a crowd began to form. Soon, the shock of the onlookers transformed into anger, and people began throwing things, smashing windows, and starting fires. The community had been forced to tolerate years of injustice and oppression, and the pent-up emotion from all those years fueled their anger. The police responded with violence as well, and eventually thousands of people from the U.S. National Guard, the Michigan State Police, and the U.S. Army were sent to Detroit to intervene. Their presence did not stem the rebellion. Thousands of people were arrested and forty-three people died, including thirty-three Black people and ten white people. More than a thousand buildings were destroyed in the fires.

After the Detroit Rebellion, even more white people moved out of the city and into the suburbs. Many buildings were never rebuilt, and the remaining residents of Detroit had to live among the physical reminders of what had happened in their community.

Once white people left the city, most people with money and power no longer thought it was worthwhile to invest in making Detroit a welcoming place to live. By the time Vincent Chin became a teenager, his city was majority poor or working-class, and the legacy of racial violence hovered over the city.

As Vincent grew older, the American car industry faced another challenge, which affected many people's job security in Detroit. Japanese cars were becoming popular. They were often more affordable and seen as more reliable than American cars, which hadn't changed as rapidly with advances in technology. Across the United States, some people were angry that money was going to Japanese car companies instead of American car companies. They were angry that American car companies were firing workers to cut back on their costs. It was common to see people who held these beliefs putting bumper stickers on their cars with anti-Japanese slogans, and some people destroyed Japanese cars with sledgehammers in protest. Rather than blaming the big companies that were responsible for the changes, many Americans blamed Japanese people instead, including Japanese Americans. It hadn't been that long since Japanese Americans were forced into internment camps during the Second World War, and the old yellow peril stereotypes of Asian people coming to steal jobs from white Americans had never really gone away. As the American auto industry declined and the city of Detroit struggled, Japanese Americans had once again become a convenient *scapegoat* for problems that people were facing. And, because many people thought all Asian Americans were essentially the same, rising anti-Japanese racism meant that anti-Asian racism was rising in general.

Businessman Charlie Cobb destroys a car in a charity campaign sponsored by northern Indiana steelworkers that allowed people to swing a sledgehammer at a Japanese-made auto for $1 a shot.

WHEN VINCENT CHIN WAS twenty-seven, he was working as a draftsman during the day and at a restaurant in Detroit's Chinatown on the weekends and in the evenings. His father had died just the previous year, and he and his mother, Lily Chin, were close. Vincent was engaged to marry his girlfriend, a Chinese American woman named Victoria Wong.

Vincent Chin.

Their future looked bright. On June 19, 1982, Vincent and a couple of his friends decided to go out to celebrate the upcoming wedding. People have different accounts about what happened next, but some of the facts are clear. Vincent and his friends were at a strip club when they got into first a verbal and then a physical fight with two white men, Ronald Ebens and his stepson Michael Nitz. Vincent Chin, his friends, and Ronald and Michael were all kicked out of the club, but the fight was not over. Ronald Ebens and Michael Nitz got in their car and were driving through the neighborhood when they spotted Vincent sitting outside of a McDonald's. There, in the street, Michael Nitz held Vincent Chin down while Ronald Ebens beat him in the head with a baseball bat. Vincent Chin died four days later. Ronald and Michael were soon arrested and charged with second-degree murder for their roles in the brutal killing.

The murder of Vincent Chin was reminiscent of the racist beatings and murders of Chinese Americans in the late 1800s. There is evidence that prejudice was behind Ronald Ebens and Michael Nitz's actions. One of the dancers at the club, a white woman named Racine Colwell, said that she heard Ronald tell Vincent and one of his friends, a Chinese American man named Jimmy Choi, "It's because of you little [m-f-s] that we are out of work." Another dancer, a Black woman named Angela (Starlene) Rudolph, said that she heard Michael call Vincent Chin "boy," a term that is used to degrade the position of men of color. Unfortunately, these comments would probably not have been surprising or unfamiliar to Vincent and his friends, but that doesn't mean they wouldn't have hurt. What was surprising, though, was what happened to Ronald Ebens and Michael Nitz.

Ronald and Michael pled guilty to the lesser charge of manslaughter and awaited their sentence from judge Charles Kaufman. Charles Kaufman decided that the two men did not have to go to jail. All they had to do was serve three years of probation and pay $3,000 in fines and $780 in court fees. Many people were shocked by the light sentence. Vincent had lost his life, and these men would only lose a few thousand dollars. Later, Charles Kaufman wrote, "These weren't the kind of men you send to jail," which made people wonder, *What "kind of men" do you send to jail, then?* It was hard not to think that the lenient sentence was only because the men were white and because Vincent was Chinese American.

Lily Chin, Vincent's mother, was furious when she heard about the judge's decision. How could her son's life be worth only $3,000? She wrote a letter to the Detroit Chinese Welfare Council, a group that, like the associations of the West Coast, sought to provide support for the city's Chinese community. Across the city, Asian Americans from many different ethnic backgrounds were quickly learning the name Vincent Chin, and they, too, were moved by the injustice of it all. One of these people was a woman named Helen Zia.

Helen Zia was a brilliant student, one of the first women to graduate from Princeton University, and an active member of the Asian American student movement of the early 1970s. Helen had been an outspoken anti-war activist and had worked to promote rights for women, people of color, and other marginalized groups. She also understood and advocated for solidarity across different groups of people. After college

Helen enrolled in medical school, but she decided she did not want to graduate. There was something else she felt she needed to do with her life. Helen Zia moved to Detroit, where she worked physically demanding jobs in construction and car manufacturing. Her awareness of social justice and solidarity had stayed with her, of course, and she was shocked by both the murder of Vincent Chin and the light sentence that Ronald Ebens and Michael Nitz received. She started to organize people around the injustice, and her writing and activism grew into a long career in journalism and advocacy. Today, Helen Zia continues to speak out for social justice and to tell Vincent Chin's story so that we never forget what happened to him.

Helen Zia at a rally for Vincent Chin in Detroit, 1983. Her sign says "Oppose all racial attacks" in both English and Chinese.

In the months after Vincent's death, Helen Zia wrote press releases that appeared in local media. She wanted to make sure that people did not forget what had happened and did not want to allow the injustice to stand. As people followed these press releases, more and more Asian American people from Detroit were inspired to do something about Vincent's death. Japanese American, Korean American, and Filipino American people showed up in solidarity with the Chinese American community. Lawyers from different Asian American backgrounds added their expertise to try to find justice for Vincent. Elders helped by hand-delivering Helen's press releases to the local newspapers. The Asian American community was energized. On March 31, 1983, a group of more than one hundred Asian American people from the Detroit area met at the Chinese Welfare Council's building to form a new organization: American Citizens for Justice (ACJ). The name they picked was sending a message that this group would stand together to advocate not only for justice in Vincent Chin's case, not only for justice in the Chinese American community, and not only for justice in the Asian American community. These Asian American citizens were making a statement that they stood for the rights of *all* Americans.

The cases against Ronald Ebens and Michael Nitz continued through both criminal and civil courts for years. Helen Zia and the Chinese American lawyer Liza Chan pushed hard for the case to be tried again, this time arguing that Vincent Chin's civil rights had been violated during the killing. In 1984, the case was retried in a federal court. Michael Nitz, who most people believed was following his stepfather's lead, was acquitted of all charges. Ronald Ebens was sentenced to twenty-five years in jail. He appealed this decision and eventually, in 1987, he too was acquitted of all charges. In 1987, Lily Chin moved back to Guangzhou, China. She had too many painful memories in Detroit. Like her great-grandfather had found, the promise of the American Dream had been much different from the reality that she had experienced.

Vincent Chin's death was a moment of awakening for many Asian Americans. Some had not known the earlier histories of oppression and resistance in Asian American communities. Others had not realized the power of solidarity across different ethnic groups. It's hard to say that harshly punishing Ronald Ebens and Michael Nitz for Vincent Chin's death would have been justice—justice would have been for Vincent Chin to never have been murdered in the first place.

Justice would be an end to racist violence of all kinds. The Asian American movement was reignited in Detroit in the 1980s, and it has continued to work for cross-racial solidarity and to promote justice for all people to this day.

LET'S THINK ABOUT THIS:

1. What movies have you seen about Chinese American people? Who played these roles? Do you think that these movies accurately depict what it means to be Chinese American? What sorts of Chinese American stories would you like to see in the media?

2. Mabel Ping-Hua Lee was only a teenager when she became an advocate for justice. She didn't have the right to vote, but she was still an active participant in American democracy. How can young people who care about justice learn from her example to take action for the causes they care about?

3. The Immigration and Nationality Act of 1965 changed the way that most Americans thought about Asian Americans. How do you typically see Asian Americans portrayed on the news or in conversations with other people?

Where have you seen or heard model minority stereotypes, and where have you seen or heard a more complete picture of Asian Americans?

4. How does learning about Vincent Chin make you feel? What would you have done if you were alive at the time and read about his death in one of Helen Zia's articles?

THE TRUTH, TODAY

In the 1980s, Chinese Americans organized with other Asian Americans to make sure that Vincent Chin's story would not be forgotten. They wanted to make sure that Americans understood the dangers of racism and that people knew that Vincent's murder was not an isolated event. They wanted to make sure people knew that America had a long history of anti-Chinese sentiment and anti-Asian violence, in the hope that this violence would never happen again. They wanted to make sure that stories of Asian American resistance and brilliance were included in the stories people tell about the country. In the following decades, however, few Americans outside of Detroit learned about Vincent Chin. His murder was not taught in most schools, and for most Americans the older histories of Chinese Americans were once again forgotten.

Then in 2020, another event reignited the Asian American movement: the Covid-19 pandemic. The virus originated in China and then rapidly spread around the world, killing millions and infecting hundreds of millions. Media commentators and politicians sometimes referred to Covid-19 as "the China virus" or used the mocking phrase the "kung flu." Suddenly, Chinese Americans were on high alert. The old yellow peril stereotypes about disease-ridden Chinese people had rapidly come back into the public consciousness. Language is powerful. Just like Japanese Americans were a convenient scapegoat for problems in the American auto industry, they feared that Chinese Americans would be a scapegoat for the pandemic. Helen Zia explained the connection to reporters in 2022: "That was what was going on in America in the 1980s. And that's why as soon as that callout in the White House was pointing the fingers at China, everybody Asian American knew that that was going to land very hard on Asians in America." The "China virus" phrase had so much power because there were old, longstanding fears about dangerous Chinese Americans that this language could attach to. And dangerous stereotypes lead to dangerous actions. Helen Zia and others who saw the connections were correct. In 2020 and the years following, racist incidents against Asian Americans surged. In 2021 alone, one in four Asian Americans reported experiencing a hate incident.

Most of the anti-Asian incidents of the 2020s have involved words. Asian American people were yelled at for bringing Covid into the country, even though they had nothing to do with it. Asian American parents reported that their young children were told by friends at school that they could not play together anymore, because of worries that they would make everyone sick. One of the most commonly reported incidents involves people telling Asian Americans to "go back to your country." These events show how the perpetual foreigner stereotype is also alive and well in the United States, because many of the targets of this language see themselves as American. Their country is the United States, yet their physical appearance makes some think that they do not and can never belong in the U.S.

Other anti-Asian incidents rose from verbal to physical attacks. These have included assaults, shootings, and elders being pushed to the ground in stores and on the streets of Chinatowns. The most well-known of these incidents was a string of killings that happened on March 16, 2021. A white man shot people at three spas in the Atlanta, Georgia, area, killing eight. Six of the people who were murdered were Asian or Asian American women. The spa murders drew national attention to the anti-Asian incidents that had been increasing for the past year. Even so, some people did not believe that these murders had anything to do with race or with Asian identity. The murderer in the spa shootings said that the women represented sexual temptation, and he was trying to eliminate that temptation. Some people took this as evidence that the killings were not about racism at all. But you, dear reader, remember history. You remember the Page Act of 1874, which barred Chinese women from entering the United States. You remember that a major justification for this act was the common stereotype that Chinese women are sexual temptresses who will corrupt white American men, and that they must be excluded to remove this temptation. So when you hear that the killer described the women as temptations, you can draw a line back through time to understand that his desire to eliminate the women is connected to racial history after all.

Not all of the verbal and physical attacks on Asian American communities can be easily traced to racist intentions, yet the sheer number of these incidents makes it clear that there is a pattern. When yellow peril stereotypes were alive and well in the 1800s, racist attacks like the Los Angeles Chinatown Massacre followed. When the language of the "China virus" reignited those stereotypes in the 2020s, racist attacks increased as well. Some people say that this language is harmless or that it's just a joke, but these examples remind us that language can have real-world effects. It is important to reject stereotypes of all kinds, even ones that other people say are only jokes.

ONCE AGAIN, every story of violence and oppression is linked to stories of resistance and solidarity. In the 1980s, Asian Americans organized together after the murder of Vincent Chin. In the 2020s, Americans from many backgrounds organized together to resist anti-Asian racism. #StopAsianHate became a common rallying cry, and thousands of people marched together to raise awareness of what was happening. The crowds at these rallies included Asian American people from all backgrounds, and they also included Americans who don't identify as Asian. People showed up in solidarity across differences to advocate for ending racism, once and for all.

A rally against anti-Asian hate crimes outside City Hall in Los Angeles, California, on March 27, 2021.

In 2021, the U.S. Congress passed something called the Covid-19 Hate Crimes Act, aimed at raising awareness of Covid-related hate crimes and making it easier to investigate these incidents. The law was introduced by two Asian American women, Representative Grace Meng and Senator Mazie Hirono, and was specifically aimed at prosecuting people who perpetuate anti-Asian hate incidents. The legislation was broadly popular. Many Asian Americans, who felt that the model minority label was hiding what was really happening, were glad to see acknowledgment of the racial terror that they were experiencing in the wake of Covid-19. At the same time, not everyone agreed with the law. Some people feared that the law put too much power in the hands of the criminal justice system, which has long played a role in the history of racial inequality. Just think of laws like the Cubic Air Ordinance, which disproportionately imprisoned Chinese American men, who then had their hair cut short while they were incarcerated. These people feared that the law would only increase the strength of the criminal justice system.

Other people pointed out that the Covid-19 Hate Crimes Act had passed barely a year into the Covid pandemic and mere months after the Atlanta spa shooting, while Black Americans had waited much longer for legislation that addressed hate crimes specifically targeting their communities to no avail. For example, in 2022, the Emmett Till Antilynching Act was passed, making lynching a federal hate crime, even though reports of anti-Black lynching are as old as the United States itself. Critics pointed out that the easier passage of a law to help Asian Americans was a reminder of the old racial hierarchy, and that Black Americans were once again made a lower priority.

Remember, the racial hierarchy hurts all people. Different groups have different experiences and different needs, and yet racism hurts all of us. If reading about this feels complicated, that's okay. We can be glad for the progress that is being made, while still wishing that more was happening. We can advocate for the rights of our own group and also advocate for the rights of others.

REMEMBER AGAIN: Wherever there are stories of racism, there are stories of strength and community. Today, more and more Asian Americans are organizing against hate. #StopAAPIHate and #StopAsianHate are viral movements, and people from all different racial backgrounds have marched, spoken up, and otherwise joined together to try to end the violence. More and more Asian Americans are recognizing that the model minority myth has ultimately harmed Asian American communities and has always upheld anti-Black racism. More people, especially young people, are speaking out against it. Asian Americans, including Chinese Americans, are fighting to have their true histories—all of their histories, the good and the bad—taught in schools and passed down from generation to generation. You, dear reader, by reading this book, are now a part of that organizing toward justice. You now have powerful knowledge. You can recognize divide and conquer, unjust laws and policies, and erasures of people's real experiences. You have examples of people, Chinese American and otherwise, who have taken action against injustice. America can be a country where all people are allowed to belong, no matter who they are or where they are from. With the knowledge you have now, what will you do to help make that America a reality?

RESOURCES FOR YOUNG READERS

Bybee, Veeda. *Li on Angel Island*. Smithsonian Historical Fiction. Bloomington, MN: Stone Arch Books, 2020.

———. *Lily and the Great Quake: A San Francisco Earthquake Survival Story*. Girls Survive. Bloomington, MN: Stone Arch Books, 2020.

Currier, Katrina S. *Kai's Journey to Gold Mountain: An Angel Island Story*. Manhattan Beach, CA: East West Discovery Press, 2005.

Freedman, Russell. *Angel Island: Gateway to Gold Mountain*. New York: Clarion Books, 2016.

Ho, Joanna. *Eyes That Kiss in the Corners*. New York: HarperCollins, 2021.

James, Helen F., and Virginia Shin-Mui Loh. *Paper Son: Lee's Journey to America*. Ann Arbor, MI: Sleeping Bear Press, 2013.

Khor, Shing Yin. *The Legend of Auntie Po*. New York: Kokila, 2021.

Lee, Milly. *Landed*. New York: Farrar, Straus and Giroux, 2006.

Leung, Julie. *Paper Son: The Inspiring Story of Tyrus Wong, Immigrant and Artist*. New York: Schwartz & Wade, 2019.

Liao, Jenny. *Everyone Loves Lunchtime but Zia*. New York: Knopf, 2023.

Shang, Wendy Wan-Long. *The Great Wall of Lucy Wu*. New York: Scholastic, 2013.

Yang, Gene Luen. *American Born Chinese*. New York: First Second, 2006.

Yang, Kelly. *Front Desk*. New York: Scholastic, 2018.

Yep, Laurence. *Dragonwings*. New York: HarperCollins, 2001.

Yoo, Paula. *From a Whisper to a Rallying Cry: The Killing of Vincent Chin and the Trial That Galvanized the Asian American Movement*. New York: Norton Young Readers, 2021.

BIBLIOGRAPHY

Alexander, Kerri Lee. "Anna May Wong: 1905–1961." National Women's History Museum. 2019. womenshistory.org/education-resources/biographies/anna-may-wong.

American Experience. "Chinese Immigrants and the Gold Rush." Accessed July 12, 2022. pbs.org/wgbh/americanexperience/features/goldrush-chinese-immigrants/.

Angel Island Immigration Station Foundation. "History of Angel Island Immigration Station." Accessed November 2, 2022. aiisf.org/history.

"Antilynching Act Signed into Law." Equal Justice Initiative. March 29, 2022. eji.org/news /antilynching-act-signed-into-law/.

"Asian Immigration: The 'Yellow Peril.'" Race in America 1880–1940. Bowling Green State University. digitalgallery.bgsu.edu/student/exhibits/show/race-in-us/asian-americans /asian-immigration-and-the--yel.

August, Linda K. "Remembering Afong Moy." The Library Company of Philadelphia. librarycompany.org/2021/02/01/remembering-afong-moy/.

Berard, Adrienne. *Water Tossing Boulders: How a Family of Chinese Immigrants Led the First Fight to Desegregate Schools in the Jim Crow South.* Boston: Beacon Press, 2016.

Blackmon, Douglas A. *Slavery by Another Name: The Re-Enslavement of Black Americans from the Civil War to World War II.* New York: Doubleday, 2008.

Blakemore, Erin. "What Was It Like to Ride the Transcontinental Railroad?" History. October 16, 2020, updated June 27, 2023. history.com/news/transcontinental-railroad -experience.

Bleiweis, Robin, Jocelyn Frye, and Rose Khattar. "Women of Color and the Wage Gap." Center for American Progress. November 17, 2021. americanprogress.org/article /women-of-color-and-the-wage-gap/.

Block, Melissa, and Elissa Nadworny. "The Legacy of the Mississippi Delta Chinese." March 18, 2017. npr.org/2017/03/18/519017287/the-legacy-of-the-mississippi-delta-chinese.

Boodhoo, Niala. "Poll: 1 Out of 4 Asian Americans Has Experienced a Hate Incident." Axios. March 30, 2021. axios.com/2021/03/30/poll-1-in-4-asian-americans-experience -hate-incident.

Britannica Kids. "California Gold Rush." Accessed July 6, 2023. kids.britannica.com /students/article/California-Gold-Rush/631740.

Budiman, Abby, and Neil R. Ruiz. "Key Facts About Asian Americans, a Diverse and Growing Population." Pew Research Center. April 29, 2021. pewresearch.org /short-reads/2021/04/29/key-facts-about-asian-americans/.

Burns, Ric, and Li-Shin Yu, directors. *The Chinese Exclusion Act.* American Experience, aired May 29, 2018, on PBS.

Cahill, Cathleen D. "Mabel Ping-Hua Lee: How Chinese-American Women Helped Shape the Suffrage Movement." Belmont-Paul Women's Equality National Monument, Women's Rights National Historical Park. National Park Service, December 14, 2020. nps.gov /articles/000/mabel-ping-hua-lee-how-chinese-american-women-helped-shape-the -suffrage-movement.htm.

California State Legislature, "Foreign Miner's License." *Social History for Every Classroom.* Accessed June 11, 2023. shec.ashp.cuny.edu/items/show/1714.

Carter, James. "The Manchu Queue: One Hairstyle to Rule Them All." The China Project. July 21, 2021. thechinaproject.com/2021/07/21/the-manchu-queue-one-hairstyle-to-rule -them-all/.

Cartwright, Mark. "Foot-Binding." World History Encyclopedia. September 27, 2017. worldhistory.org/Foot-Binding/.

Case No. 6,546, Circuit Court, D. California 12 F. Cas. 252; 1879 U.S. App. LEXIS 1629; 5 Sawy. 552; 13 West. Jur. 409; 20 Alb. Law J. 250; 25 Int. Rev. Rec. 312.

CBS San Francisco. "San Jose Apologizes Over 1887 Chinatown Destruction, Racism Against Chinese Community—'Acknowledge the History.'" CBS News. September 29, 2021. cbsnews.com/sanfrancisco/news/san-jose-chinese-community-apology-1887 -chinatown-destruction/.

Center for Labor Education & Research University of Hawai'i—West O'ahu. "History of Labor in Hawai'i." Accessed August 20, 2022. hawaii.edu/uhwo/clear/home /HawaiiLaborHistory.html.

Central Pacific Railroad Photographic History Museum. "Chinese-American Contribution to Transcontinental Railroad." Accessed August 20, 2022. cprr.org/Museum/Chinese.html.

Chang, Gordon H. "Op-Ed: Remember the Chinese Immigrants Who Built America's First Transcontinental Railroad." *Los Angeles Times,* May 10, 2019.

Chang, Gordon H., and Shelley F. Fishkin. *The Chinese and the Iron Road: Building the Transcontinental Railroad.* Redwood City, CA: Stanford University Press, 2019.

Chang, Rachel. "When 20,000 Asian Americans Demanded Garment Workers' Rights— And Won." History. April 30, 2021. history.com/news/garment-workers-strike-chinatown.

Chelsey, Kate. "First Transcontinental Railroad and Stanford Forever Linked." Stanford News. May 8, 2019. news.stanford.edu/2019/05/08/first-transcontinental-railroad -stanford-forever-linked/.

Chen, Michelle. "'She Could Have Been Your Mother': Anti-Asian Racism a Year after Atlanta Spa Shootings." *The Guardian.* March 16, 2022. theguardian.com/us-news/2022 /mar/16/anti-asian-racism-atlanta-spa-shootings-anniversary.

Chesley, Frank. "Chinese Exclusion Repeal Act, Aka the Magnuson Act, Is Signed on December 17, 1943." History Link. April 24, 2009. historylink.org/File/8993.

"The Chinese Massacre: One of Los Angeles' Worst Atrocities." PBS. October 17, 2017. Video, pbs.org/video/the-chinese-massacre-one-of-los-angeles-worst-atrocities/.

"The Chinese Six Companies." American Experience. Video, pbs.org/wgbh /americanexperience/features/plague-golden-gate-chinese-six-companies/.

Chionsini, James. "Ho Ah Kow V. Nunan." FoundSF. Accessed May 31, 2023. foundsf.org /index.php?title=Ho_Ah_Kow_v._Nunan.

Chiou-Ling Yeh. "'A Saga of Democracy': Toy Len Goon, American Mother of the Year, and the Cultural Cold War." *Pacific Historical Review* 81, no. 3 (2012): 432–61. doi.org/10 .1525/phr.2012.81.3.432.

Chishti, Muzaffar, Faye Hipsman, and Isabel Ball. "Fifty Years On, the 1965 Immigration and Nationality Act Continues to Reshape the United States." Migration Policy Institute. October 15, 2015. migrationpolicy.org/article/fifty-years-1965-immigration-and -nationality-act-continues-reshape-united-states.

Choy, Catherine C. *Asian American Histories of the United States.* Boston: Beacon Press, 2022.

Davis, Nancy E. *The Chinese Lady: Afong Moy in Early America.* New York: Oxford University Press, 2019.

Davis, Wynne. "Vincent Chin Was Killed 40 Years Ago. Here's Why His Case Continues to Resonate." NPR. June 19, 2022. npr.org/2022/06/19/1106118117/vincent-chin-aapi -hate-incidents.

DeVito, Lee. "Nearly 40 Years Ago, a Metro Times Reporter Helped Turn the Killing of Vincent Chin into a Movement for Asian American Rights." *Detroit Metro Times,* June 22, 2022. metrotimes.com/news/nearly-40-years-ago-a-metro-times-reporter -helped-turn-the-killing-of-vincent-chin-into-a-movement-for-asian-american-rights -30361928.

Dhillon, Hardeep. "How the Fight for Birthright Citizenship Shaped the History of Asian American Families." Untold Stories of American History. *Smithsonian Magazine,* March 27, 2023. smithsonianmag.com/history/how-the-fight-for-birthright-citizenship-reshaped -asian-american-families-180981866/.

Do, Anh. "How One Woman Fought Bigotry and Helped Change the Way Asian Americans See Themselves." *Los Angeles Times,* May 24, 2023. latimes.com/california/story /2023-05-24/helen-zia-civil-rights-lgbtq-anti-asian-violence.

"Dogan Goon in U.S. Army Uniform, Ca. 1918." Maine Memory Network. Maine Historical Society. Accessed June 19, 2022. mainememory.net/artifact/10366.

"Dr. Mabel Ping-Hua Lee." National Park Service. March 9, 2022. nps.gov/people /mabel-lee.htm.

Duignan, Brian. "Plessy v. Ferguson." Britannica. June 21, 2023. britannica.com/event /Plessy-v-Ferguson-1896.

The Editors of Encyclopaedia Britannica. "Central Pacific Railroad." Britannica. April 28, 2023. britannica.com/topic/Central-Pacific-Railroad.

———. "Chinese Civil War." Britannica. January 12, 2018. britannica.com/event/Chinese -Civil-War.

———. "Cold War." Britannica. June 20, 2023. britannica.com/event/Cold-War.

———. "Radical Reconstruction." Britannica. January 30, 2022. britannica.com/topic /Radical-Reconstruction.

———. "Second Sino-Japanese War." Britannica. November 10, 2020. britannica.com/event /Second-Sino-Japanese-War.

Egan, Charles. *Voices of Angel Island: Inscriptions and Immigrant Poetry, 1910–1945.* New York: Bloomsbury Academic, 2022.

Encinas, Jorge. "There's a Long, Ignominious Trail of Bans, Registries and Forced Relocation." NPR. Code Switch. February 2, 2017. npr.org/sections /codeswitch/2017/02/02/512903229/theres-a-long-ignominious-trail-of-bans-registries -forced-relocation.

"Equal Pay for Asian American, Native Hawaiian, and Pacific Islander Women." National Asian Pacific American Women's Forum. Accessed July 2, 2023. napawf.org/equalpay.

Eschner, Kat. "Chop Suey: An American Classic." *Smithsonian Magazine.* August 29, 2017. smithsonianmag.com/smart-news/chop-suey-american-classic-180964610/.

Facing History & Ourselves. "Paper Sons and Daughters and the Complexity of Choices During the Exclusion Era." January 12, 2023. facinghistory.org/resource-library/paper -sons-daughters-complexity-choices-during-exclusion-era.

Fang, Karen. "No. 3216: Internment Camp Art Schools." Engines of Our Ingenuity. December 10, 2019. uh.edu/engines/epi3216.htm.

Farkas, Lani A. T., and Adrian Praetzellis. " 'Bury My Bones in California;' History and Archaeology of Yee Ah Tye." Anthropological Studies Center, Sonoma State University, 2000.

Fuchs, Chris. "150 Years Ago, Chinese Railroad Workers Staged the Era's Largest Labor Strike." NBC News. June 21, 2017. nbcnews.com/news/asian-america/150-years-ago -chinese-railroad-workers-staged-era-s-largest-n774901.

Gandhi, Lakshmi. "The Transcontinental Railroad's Dark Costs: Exploited Labor, Stolen Lands." History. October 8, 2021. history.com/news/transcontinental-railroad-workers -impact.

Gandhi, Lakshmi. "What Does 'Sold Down the River' Really Mean? The Answer Isn't Pretty." NPR: Code Switch. January 27, 2014. npr.org/sections /codeswitch/2014/01/27/265421504/what-does-sold-down-the-river-really-mean-the -answer-isnt-pretty.

The Gilder Lehrman Institute of American History. "Transcontinental Railroad Fact Sheet." 2014. gilderlehrman.org/sites/default/files/inline-pdfs/Transcontinental%20Railroad%20 Fact%20Sheet.pdf.

Gong Lum v. Rice, 275 U.S. 78, 48 S. Ct. 91 (1927).

Gonzales, Richard. "Rebuilding Chinatown After the 1906 Quake." NPR: Morning Edition. April 12, 2006. npr.org/2006/04/12/5337215/rebuilding-chinatown-after-the-1906 -quake.

Gooden, Mark A. "Gong Lum V. Rice." Britannica. November 14, 2022. britannica.com /event/Gong-Lum-v-Rice.

Gray, Horace, and Supreme Court of the United States. *U.S. Reports: Fong Yue Ting v. United States, 149 U.S. 698*. 1892. Periodical. loc.gov/item/usrep149698/.

"The Great 1906 San Francisco Earthquake." United States Geological Survey. Accessed January 4, 2023. earthquake.usgs.gov/earthquakes/events/1906calif/18april/.

Heath, Erle. "A Railroad Record That Defies Defeat." *Southern Pacific Bulletin XVI*, no. 5 (1928): 3–5.

Hinnershitz, Stephanie. "The Chinese Exclusion Act." Bill of Rights Institute. Accessed January 4, 2023. billofrightsinstitute.org/essays/the-chinese-exclusion-act.

History Colorado. "The Rise and Fall of Denver's Chinatown." April 11, 2019. historycolorado.org/story/colorado-voices/2019/04/11/rise-and-fall-denvers-chinatown.

History.com Editors. "Asian American Milestones: Timeline." World History Encyclopedia. March 22, 2021, updated April 28, 2023. history.com/topics/immigration/asian -american-timeline.

———. "Black Codes." History. June 1, 2010, updated March 29, 2023. history.com/topics /black-history/black-codes.

———. "Chinese Miners Are Massacred in Wyoming Territory." History. November 16, 2009, updated April 3, 2021. history.com/this-day-in-history/whites-massacre-chinese-in -wyoming-territory.

———. "Cultural Revolution." History. November 9, 2009, updated April 3, 2020. history.com/topics/asian-history/cultural-revolution.

———. "Japanese Internment Camps." History. October 29, 2009, updated October 29, 2021. history.com/topics/world-war-ii/japanese-american-relocation.

———. "Transcontinental Railroad." April 20, 2010, updated September 11, 2019. history.com/topics/inventions/transcontinental-railroad.

———. "U.S. Immigration Since 1965." History. March 5, 2010, updated June 7, 2019. history.com/topics/immigration/us-immigration-since-1965.

History.com Staff. "Chinese Exclusion Act." History. August 24, 2018, updated August 9, 2022. history.com/topics/19th-century/chinese-exclusion-act-1882.

Howe, Marvine. "Chinatown Exhibit Honors the Hard Lot of the Laundryman." *New York Times,* December 12, 1984.

Hsu, Madeline Y. *The Good Immigrants: How the Yellow Peril Became the Model Minority.* Princeton, NJ: Princeton University Press, 2017.

Hua, Vanessa. "Golden Spike Redux." National Parks Conservation Association. Summer 2019. npca.org/articles/2192-golden-spike-redux.

"Immigrant Voices." Angel Island Immigration Station Foundation. immigrant-voices.aiisf.org/.

"Immigration and Nationality Act of 1965." History, Art & Archives. U.S. House of Representatives, Accessed January 4, 2023. history.house.gov/Historical-Highlights /1951-2000/Immigration-and-Nationality-Act-of-1965/.

Jin, Connie Hanzhang. "6 Charts That Dismantle the Trope of Asian Americans as a Model Minority." NPR. May 25, 2021. npr.org/2021/05/25/999874296/6-charts-that -dismantle-the-trope-of-asian-americans-as-a-model-minority.

Jung, John. *Chopsticks in the Land of Cotton: Lives of Mississippi Delta Chinese Grocers.* N.p.: Yin & Yang Press, 2011.

Kambhampaty, Anna P. "In 1968, These Activists Coined the Term 'Asian American'—And Helped Shape Decades of Advocacy." *Time.* May 22, 2020. time.com/5837805/asian american history/.

Karlamangla, Soumya. "Anna May Wong Will Be the First Asian American on U.S. Currency." *New York Times,* October 18, 2022.

Katz, Jonathan M. "Birth of a Birthright." *Politico Magazine.* October 31, 2018. politico .com/magazine/story/2018/10/31/birthright-citizenship-wong-kim-ark-222098/.

Kaur, Harmeet. "Vincent Chin Was Beaten to Death 40 Years Ago. His Case Is Still Relevant Today." History Refocused. CNN, June 23, 2022. cnn.com/2022/06/23/us/vincent-chin -death-40-anniversary-cec/index.html.

Kay, Lai Y. Y., A Yup Lai Foon, and Chung Leong. *The Chinese Question from a Chinese Standpoint.* Pamphlet. 1874. americainclass.org/wp-content/uploads/2014/07 /ChineseQuestion-FullText.pdf.

Kim, Claire J. "The Racial Triangulation of Asian Americans." *Politics & Society 27,* no. 1 (March 1999): 105–138.

Kim, Philip. "A History of the Invisible Mississippi Delta Chinese Community." BuzzFeed. May 26, 2022. buzzfeed.com/philipkim/mississippi-delta-chinese-community-history.

Klein, Christopher. "The Chinese Immigrant Son Who Fought for Birthright Citizenship." History. May 30, 2017, updated March 18, 2021. history.com/news/born-in-the-usa-the -immigrant-son-who-fought-for-birthright-citizenship.

Kuperberg, Clara, and Julia Kuperberg, directors. *Yellowface: Asian Whitewashing and Racism in Hollywood.* Wichita Films, 2018.

"Labor Organizing Changed the Hawaiian Islands Forever." *The American Postal Worker,* May/June 2003.

The Learning Network. "Jan. 17, 1893 | Hawaiian Monarchy Overthrown by America- Backed Businessmen." *New York Times,* January 17, 2012.

Lee, Erika. *At America's Gates: Chinese Immigration during the Exclusion Era, 1882–1943.* Chapel Hill: University of North Carolina Press, 2003.

——. *The Making of Asian America: A History.* New York: Simon & Schuster, 2016.

Lee, Gordon. "The Forgotten Revolution." *Hyphen,* no. 1. June 1, 2003. hyphenmagazine .com/magazine/issue-1-premiere-summer-2003/forgotten-revolution.

Lew-Williams, Beth. *The Chinese Must Go: Violence, Exclusion, and the Making of the Alien in America.* Cambridge, MA: Harvard University Press, 2018.

Library of Congress. "From Gold Rush to Golden State." Accessed July 3, 2023. loc.gov /collections/california-first-person-narratives/articles-and-essays/early-california-history /from-gold-rush-to-golden-state/.

——. "Hawaii: Life in a Plantation Society." Classroom Materials. Accessed January 3, 2023. loc.gov/classroom-materials/immigration/japanese/hawaii-life-in-a-plantation -society/.

——. "Immigration and Relocation in U.S. History." Classroom Materials. Accessed July 3, 2023. loc.gov/classroom-materials/immigration/.

Lienhard, John H. "No. 1028: Fusang." Engines of Our Ingenuity. University of Houston, Accessed January 23, 2023. uh.edu/engines/epi1028.htm.

"Life Story: Anna May Wong (1905–1961)." Women and the American Story. Accessed January 4, 2023. wams.nyhistory.org/confidence-and-crises/jazz-age/anna-may -wong/.

Linda Hall Library. "Bridges and Tunnels on the Transcontinental Railroad." Accessed August 20, 2022. railroad.lindahall.org/essays/tunnels-bridges.html.

Linda Hall Library. "Snow Sheds: How the CPRR Crossed the Summit." Accessed August 20, 2022. railroad.lindahall.org/essays/innovations.html.

Little, Becky. "How the 1982 Murder of Vincent Chin Ignited a Push for Asian American Rights." History. May 5, 2020. history.com/news/vincent-chin-murder-asian-american-rights.

Lockwood, Matthew. "A Lesson for American Foreign Trade with China." Yale University Press. January 6, 2020. yalebooks.yale.edu/2020/01/06/a-lesson-for-american-foreign-trade-with-china/.

Loh-Hagan, Virginia, Jing Kwoh, Jayson Chang, and Pat Kwoh. "Excluded from History: The Page Act of 1875." *Social Education* 86, no. 2 (March/April 2022).

Louie, Andrea. "From Chinese Laundress to Mother of the Year: Bringing the Story of Toy Len Goon Beyond the Model Minority Myth." Maine Historical Society, June 24, 2021.

Luo, Michael. "America Was Eager for Chinese Immigrants. What Happened?" *The New Yorker,* August 23, 2021.

Malleck, Julia. "The U.S. Mint Gave Hollywood Legend Anna May Wong Long Overdue Recognition." Quartz. October 21, 2022. qz.com/the-us-mint-gave-hollywood-legend-anna-may-wong-long-ov-1849688398.

Mass Moments. "Chinese Workers Arrive in North Adams." MassHumanities. Accessed June 13, 2023. massmoments.org/moment-details/chinese-workers-arrive-in-north-adams.html.

Mathews, Jay. "China's Columbus." *Washington Post,* July 12, 1980.

Miles, Hannah. "WWII Propaganda: The Influence of Racism." *Artifacts Journal,* no. 6 (March 2012). artifactsjournal.missouri.edu/2012/03/wwii-propaganda-the-influence-of-racism/.

Mintz, S., and S. McNeil. "Building the Transcontinental Railroad." Digital History. 2018. www.digitalhistory.uh.edu/disp_textbook.cfm?smtID=2&psid=3147.

———. "Chinese Immigrants and the Building of the Transcontinental Railroad." Digital History. 2018. www.digitalhistory.uh.edu/voices/china1.cfm.

Morgan, Thaddeus. "How Hollywood Cast White Actors in Caricatured Asian Roles." History. August 20, 2018, updated May 5, 2023. history.com/news/yellowface-whitewashing-in-film-america.

Murphy, Edward D. "Celebrated Chinese American Mom to Be Honored Posthumously in Portland." *Portland Press Herald,* September 30, 2021.

National Archives. "Chinese Exclusion Act (1882)." Milestone Documents. January 17, 2023. archives.gov/milestone-documents/chinese-exclusion-act.

———. "The 1897 Petition Against the Annexation of Hawaii." Educator Resources. November 24, 2021. archives.gov/education/lessons/hawaii-petition#background.

———. "The Great Migration (1910–1970)." June 28, 2021. archives.gov/research/african-americans/migrations/great-migration.

———. "Joint Address to Congress Leading to a Declaration of War Against Japan (1941)." Milestone Documents. February 8, 2022. archives.gov/milestone-documents/joint-address-to-congress-declaration-of-war-against-japan.

"The New Foreign Miners Tax Law." *Sacramento Daily Union,* May 10, 1852. cdnc.ucr.edu/cgi-bin/cdnc?a=d&d=SDU18520510.2.4&e=------en—20--1--txt-txIN-------.

News Source. "Today In History: 14 February 1779—Capt James Cook Is Killed by Hawaiians at Kealakekua Bay." *Samoa Global News,* February 14, 2022. samoaglobalnews.com/today-in-history-14-february-1779-capt-james-cook-is-killed-by-hawaiians-at-kealakekua-bay/.

Ngai, Mae. *The Chinese Question: The Gold Rushes and Global Politics.* New York: W. W. Norton, 2021.

Nomiyama, Courtney. "Belonging On and Off the Battlefield: Asian Americans in the U.S.

Military." Library of Congress. Accessed January 4, 2023. loc.gov/ghe/cascade/index.html ?appid=6301eee806184a9c885374869c325ba4.

"Page Act, 1875." Women and the American Story. Accessed January 4, 2023. wams.nyhistory.org/industry-and-empire/expansion-and-empire/page-act-1875/.

Park, Hannah. " 'A Sad and Glorious History': One of NYC's Last Chinese Hand Laundries Closes." NBC News. October 9, 2020. nbcnews.com/specials/one-of-new-york-city-last -chinese-hand-laundries-closes/.

Pilgrim, David. "What Was Jim Crow." Jim Crow Museum. jimcrowmuseum.ferris.edu /what.htm.

Plessy v. Ferguson, 163 U.S. 537 (1896).

"Plessy v. Ferguson." Oyez. Accessed June 17, 2023. oyez.org/cases/1850-1900/163us537.

Poston, Dudley L., Michael Xinxiang Mao, and Mei-Yu Yu. "The Global Distribution of the Overseas Chinese Around 1990." *Population and Development Review* 20, no. 3 (1994): 631–45. doi.org/10.2307/2137606.

Pu'ukoholā Heiau National Historic Site. "Kamehameha the Great." National Park Service. April 27, 2023. nps.gov/puhe/learn/historyculture/kamehameha.htm.

Qianlong. "Letter To George III, 1793." USC US-China Institute. December 13, 1901. china.usc.edu/emperor-qianlong-letter-george-iii-1793.

Reuters Staff. "Fact Check: Quotes from Prominent American Statesmen on Race Are Accurate." Reuters. July 6, 2020. reuters.com/article/uk-factcheck-quotes-statesmen -race/fact-check-quotes-from-prominent-american-statesmen-on-race-are-accurate -idUSKBN2471YA.

Rifkin, Glenn. "Overlooked No More: Homer Plessy, Who Sat on a Train and Stood Up for Civil Rights." *New York Times,* January 31, 2020.

Rojas, Leslie B. "Who Was Wong Kim Ark? How a Son of Immigrants Helped Define Who Is a U.S. Citizen." 89.3 KPCC. January 19, 2011. archive.kpcc.org/blogs/multiamerican /2011/01/19/7987/who-was-wong-kim-ark/.

Rotondi, Jessica P. "Before the Chinese Exclusion Act, This Anti-Immigrant Law Targeted Asian Women." History. March 19, 2021. history.com/news/chinese-immigration-page-act-women.

Ruiz, Neil G., Luis Noe-Bustamante, and Sono Shah. "Diverse Cultures and Shared Experiences Shape Asian American Identities." Pew Research Center. May 8, 2023. pewresearch.org/race-ethnicity/2023/05/08/diverse-cultures-and-shared-experiences -shape-asian-american-identities/.

Sayej, Nadja. " 'Forgotten by Society'—How Chinese Migrants Built the Transcontinental Railroad." *Guardian,* July 18, 2019. theguardian.com/artanddesign/2019/jul/18 /forgotten-by-society-how-chinese-migrants-built-the-transcontinental-railroad.

Schaetzl, Randall J., Giles T. Severin, and Robert A. Muller. "Mississippi River." Britannica. June 19, 2023. britannica.com/place/Mississippi-River.

Seppa, Nathan. "Metropolitan Life on the Mississippi." *Washington Post,* March 12, 1997.

Serdiukov, Stepan. "White Landowners in Hawaii Imported Russian Workers in the Early 1900s, to Dilute the Labor Power of Asians in the Islands." The Conversation. November 29, 2022. theconversation.com/white-landowners-in-hawaii-imported-russian-workers-in -the-early-1900s-to-dilute-the-labor-power-of-asians-in-the-islands-192387.

SFSD History Research Project. "Sheriff Matthew Nunan and the Chinese Queues." Accessed November 12, 2022. sfsdhistory.com/eras/sheriff-matthew-nunan-and-the -chinese-queues.

Shyong, Frank. "History Forgot the 1871 Los Angeles Chinese Massacre, but We've All Been Shaped by Its Violence." *Los Angeles Times,* October 24, 2021.

Smith, Marian L. "INS Administration of Racial Provisions in U.S. Immigration and Nationality Law Since 1898." *Prologue Magazine* 34, no. 2 (2002). archives.gov /publications/prologue/2002/summer/immigration-law-1.

Soule, Frank, John H. Gihon, and James Nisbet. *The Annals of San Francisco*. New York: D. Appleton & Company, 1855.

Sprunt, Barbara. "Here's What the New Hate Crimes Law Aims to Do as Attacks on Asian Americans Rise." NPR. May 20, 2021. npr.org/2021/05/20/998599775/biden-to-sign the-covid-19-hate-crimes-bill-as-anti-asian-american-attacks-rise.

Stinton, Eric. "Remembering the Chinese Plantation Workers, Hawaii's First Foreign Contract Laborers." January 3, 2020. khon2.com/remembering-hawaii/remembering-the -chinese-plantation-workers-hawaiis-first-foreign-contract-laborers/.

Sur, Wilma. "Hawaiʻi's Masters and Servants Act: Brutal Slavery?" *The Archival Collections at the University of Hawaiʻi School of Law Library*, 2008.

Tajima-Peña, Renee, and Christine Choy, directors. *Who Killed Vincent Chin?* POV, 1989.

Thornton, Stuart. "Gold Fever." National Geographic Education. May 20, 2022. education.nationalgeographic.org/resource/gold-fever/.

Tom, Pamela, director. *American Masters: Tyrus*. American Masters, 2017.

Tonge, Peter. "Natchez: In 1850 Half of the Millionaires in the US Lived Here." *Christian Science Monitor*, March 22, 1983.

Twain, Mark. "Honolulu, September 10, 1866." *Sacramento Daily Union*, September 26, 1866.

Tucker, William H. "The Ideology of Racism: Misusing Science to Justify Racial Discrimination." UN Chronicle. Accessed January 3, 2023. un.org/en/chronicle/article /ideology-racism-misusing-science-justify-racial-discrimination.

Ulysses S. Grant National Historic Site. "Ulysses S. Grant, Chinese Immigration, and the Page Act of 1875." National Park Service. Accessed January 4, 2023. nps.gov/articles/000 /ulysses-s-grant-chinese-immigration-and-the-page-act-of-1875.htm.

United States v. Wong Kim Ark, 169 U.S. 649 (1898).

Union Pacific Railroad Museum. "The Summit Tunnel." Accessed August 20, 2022. uprrmuseum.org/uprrm/exhibits/curators-corner/summit-tunnel/index.htm.

University of Hawaii Professional Assembly. "Lessons from Hawaii's History of Organized Labor." March 29, 2021. uhpa.org/monday-report/dont-let-history-repeat-itself/.

Urofsky, Melvin I. "Homer Plessy: American Shoemaker." Britannica. March 13, 2023. britannica.com/biography/Homer-Plessy.

VOA News. "Museum of Chinese in America Shows a Little-Known History." November 3, 2010. voanews.com/a/museum-of-chinese-in-americas-shows-a-little-known-history -106736769/163418.html.

Wade, Lizzie. "The Ghosts in the Museum." Science. July 8, 2021. science.org/content /article/racist-scientist-built-collection-human-skulls-should-we-still-study-them.

Wallace, Kelly. "Forgotten Los Angeles History: The Chinese Massacre of 1871." Los Angeles Public Library. May 19, 2017. lapl.org/collections-resources/blogs/lapl/chinese -massacre-1871.

Wallenfeldt, Jeff. "Angel Island Immigration Station." Britannica. October 3, 2019. britannica.com/topic/Angel-Island-Immigration-Station.

Wang, Frances Kai-Hwa. "Who Is Vincent Chin? The History and Relevance of a 1982 Killing." NBC News. June 15, 2017. nbcnews.com/news/asian-america/who-vincent-chin -history-relevance-1982-killing-n771291.

"Water to Paper, Paint to Sky: The Art of Tyrus Wong." Walt Disney Family Museum. Accessed January 4, 2023. waltdisney.org/exhibitions/water-paper-paint-sky-art-tyrus -wong.

Wey, Nancy. "Chinese Americans in California," in *Five Views: An Ethnic Historic Site Survey for California*. California Department of Parks and Recreation, Office of Historic Preservation, 1988.

What shall we do with John Chinaman? 2 illustrations: 1. Irishman throwing a Chinese man

over cliff towards China; 2. Southern plantation owner leading him to cotton fields. 1869.
Photograph. loc.gov/item/2001696535/.

Wilson, Charles R. "Chinese in Mississippi: An Ethnic People in a Biracial Society."
Mississippi History Now. November 2002. mshistorynow.mdah.ms.gov/issue/mississippi
-chinese-an-ethnic-people-in-a-biracial-society.

Wong, Hansi Lo. "Chinese-American Descendants Uncover Forged Family Histories." NPR:
Code Switch. December 17, 2013. npr.org/sections/codeswitch/2013/12/17/251833652
/chinese-american-descendants-uncover-forged-family-history.

Wong, Vivian Wu. "Somewhere between White and Black: The Chinese in Mississippi."
OAH Magazine of History 10, no. 4 (Summer 1996): 33–36. jstor.org/stable/25163098.

Wu, Nina. "A Retelling of Gold Rush History: The Lives of Chinese Miners." Inside
Oakland. Accessed December 20, 2022. projects.journalism.berkeley.edu/oakland/culture
/ninagr.html.

Xi, Luo, and Ella N. Wu. "Historical Record of Chinese Americans: Why Early Chinese-
American Immigrants Were Subject to the Laundry Industry." The Association of Chinese
Americans for Social Justice. April 22, 2021. usdandelion.com/archives/4592.

Yang, Jia Lynn. "Overlooked No More: Mabel Ping-Hua Lee, Suffragist With a Distinction."
New York Times, September 19, 2020. nytimes.com/2020/09/19/obituaries/mabel-ping
-hua-lee-overlooked.html.

Yang, Joshua S. "The Anti-Chinese Cubic Air Ordinance." *American Journal of Public Health*
99, no. 3 (March 2009). ajph.aphapublications.org/doi/10.2105/AJPH.2008.145813.

Yee, Amy. "Stephen Park On Playing A Code-Switching Character In Steinbeck's 'East
Of Eden.'" NPR: Code Switch. November 3, 2015. npr.org/sections/codeswitch
/2015/11/03/453981918/stephen-park-on-playing-a-code-switching-character-in
-steinbecks-cast-of-eden.

Yoo, Paula. *From a Whisper to a Rallying Cry: The Killing of Vincent Chin and the Trial That
Galvanized the Asian American Movement.* New York: Norton Young Readers, 2021.

Young, Patrick. "When a Ban on the Chinese Was Proposed and Frederick Douglass Spoke
Out." Long Island Wins. February 8, 2017. longislandwins.com/columns/immigrants
-civil-war/ban-chinese-proposed-frederick-douglass-spoke-3/.

Zelin, Madeleine, and Sue Gronewold. "Macartney and the Emperor." Asia for Educators,
Columbia University. Accessed February 19, 2023. afe.easia.columbia.edu/special/china
_1750_macartney.htm.

Zhou, Min. "Asians in America: The Paradox of 'The Model Minority' and 'The Perpetual
Foreigner.'" 43rd Annual Sorokin Lecture at University of Saskatchewan, Saskatoon,
Saskatchewan, Canada, February 9, 2012.

Zia, Helen. *Asian American Dreams: The Emergence of an American People.* New York:
Farrar, Straus and Giroux, 2000.

Zwonitzer, Mark, and Michael Chin, directors. *Transcontinental Railroad.* American
Experience, 2003.

IMAGE CREDITS